ALBERT EINSTEIN
and PHYSICS

Order this book online at www.trafford.com
or email orders@trafford.com

Most Trafford titles are also available at major online book retailers.

Printed in the United States of America.

ISBN: 978-1-4251-7205-3 (sc)
ISBN: 978-1-4251-7206-0 (e)

Library of Congress Control Number: 2012918267

Trafford rev. 09/12/2013

www.trafford.com

North America & international
toll-free: 1 888 232 4444 (USA & Canada)
fax: 812 355 4082

For
My Father who taught me to work
My Grandmother who taught me to save
My Mother who taught me to love music
God that upheld and blessed me
Bob

For
My wonderful, beautiful wife, Loree
My three lovely daughters
My precious grandchildren
Ivan

For
My husband, Wieslaw Nowak, Polish artist
My son, Paul Nowak, professional Ph.D.
My daughter, Agnieszka Nowak, M.D.
Barbara

CONTENTS

FORWARD

This book touches only the surface of the subjects presented. Books and articles are written on these subjects by those studying, working and publishing in these areas. For in-depth knowledge, delve into the past and current works, and recent publications. Enjoy this book as a path into the great field of physics.

PREFACE

What was–<u>WAS</u>,
What is–<u>IS</u>,
What will be-<u>WILL BE</u>!

In the beginning, God created a singularity and expanded it creating light. In God's time, elements developed into universes, galaxies, suns, planets, stars, and the Good Earth. In the later, there was day and night as it rotated, and then God formed water for oceans, lakes, rivers and streams; and created all of life, plants and animals, including human beings.

So it was and so it is.

INTRODUCTION

RELATIVITY, QUANTUM, ENERGY-MASS, SPACE-TIME, FIELD, and ATOM were explored and contributed to by Albert Einstein, and published in his books and writings. These concepts are here briefly mentioned or defined:

Relativity is the easiest to correlate with Einstein's books: *Relativity, The Special and General Theory* (1905) is referred to as the special theory of relativity, and *The Meaning of Relativity Including the Relativistic Theory of the Non-Symmetric Field* (1916) is referred to as the general theory of relativity. To the general theory of relativity, Appendix I was added in 1921 and Appendix II was added in 1954. Einstein's special and general theories of relativity helped change the development of physics.

Quantum is defined by Planck in 1900. He stressed that energy from any mass, released or added, is by energy bursts he termed quanta. The quantum theory's groundwork was added to by Einstein. So far, it has grown to include quantum mechanics, quantum electrodynamics and quantum chromo-dynamics.

Energy-mass is bound together by Einstein's equation $E=mc^2$ of 1905. Einstein's equation expresses the equivalence of mass and energy. E stands for energy, m stands for mass, and c^2 is the speed of light squared. The Dirac-Einstein revision, $E=\pm mc^2$, is more correct mathematically. $E=mc^2$ is well known throughout the world, and it is used in appropriate mathematical problems, solutions of the universe, and scientific concepts at every opportunity.

Space-time was presented by Einstein in 1905 in his special theory of relativity. Einstein's important concept of space-time was a four dimensional unification of three of space (length, width, and height) and one of time.

Field. Einstein used the field concept discovered by Faraday that Einstein described as a remarkable advancement in scientific logic. The major usage that Einstein made was to change all particles and materialistic points to fields.

Atom. An atom has a nucleus surrounded by orbiting electrons. (The hydrogen atom has only one electron.) The nucleus contains protons and neutrons. Einstein accepted Bohr's classical atom since its introduction in 1913. With the passing of time, progress has been made with the concentration of work on the atom in the microsciences.

Chapter 1

MECHANICAL THEORIES vs. FIELD THEORIES

In the seventeenth to nineteenth centuries, physicists were primarily concerned with heat, magnetism and electricity, and their experimentation and exploration was largely quantitative and mechanical, and a search for scientific laws. Gradually there was a change to qualitative and mathematical physics because of improvements in the precision of scientific instruments and increasing professionalism. Science in the 1890s and the early 1900s changed through techniques and new theories shaping physics as it is known today based on the work of dedicated scientists who preceded them.

In 1665, Newton wrote one of the most important books at the time, *Principia*, which contained his three laws of motion. The first law is Galileo's concept of inertia which Newton refined; the second law is the relationship of acceleration to force and inertia; and the third law is interaction of one item to another in action and reaction.

In 1675, Roemer is accredited with the first rough estimate of the speed of light that he accomplished by measuring the time required for light to travel between Jupiter and the earth. This was important because it showed light had a finite speed.

Newton's particle theory of light was accepted by most scientists, but in 1678, Huygens presented his wave motion of light. Using his wave motion principle, Huygens explained the law of reflection and refraction. It took time for scientists to agree

1

that Huygens was correct. In 1681, Huygens invented the achromatic eyepiece for telescopes.

In 1687, Newton published a paper on mathematical principles that represented a change in the use of mathematics in the seventeenth century. Visual representation was replaced by mathematical equations. European mathematicians, including Euler, used mathematical analysis in mechanical problems using a different calculus which proved successful in their solutions.

In the 1700s, ether was widely used in research as it transmitted transverse vibrations. Using his theory, Euler helped explain ideas of ether transmission, magnetic and electrical forces, and gravitation of heat and light. Euler's theory of light was based on mathematics. Euler was instrumental in promoting the use of higher mathematics especially calculus, trigonometry and analytical mathematics. In 1706, Euler popularized the Greek letter pi to stand for the ratio of a circle's circumference to its diameter, which was the work of Archimedes who correctly determined Antiphon's work in the third century B.C.

In 1750, Wright, when viewing through an improved telescope, determined that more stars were seen clustered together when looking in one direction than in other directions.

In 1781, Herschel and his sister, Caroline, discovered the planet Uranus. They also spotted pinpoints of lights within certain nebulae in clouds of gas or dust. In 1787, Herschel built a reflecting telescope, and he detected infrared radiation from the sun in 1800.

In 1814, lens manufacturer, von Fraunhofer, was testing a lens in artificial light, and he wanted to check it in sunlight also. He was only checking for imperfections in his lens that he used in his lamps to give off heat or light. Von Fraunhofer noticed and studied the absorption lines in the solar spectrums of colored light he obtained in checking his lens, and he called them Fraunhofer lines.

In 1819, Oersted, while giving a lecture demonstration, moved a wire with an electric current near a compass which moved the compass' needle. Oersted realized his carelessness of moving an electric current near a magnetic field produced something different, and it turned out to be the beginning of the understanding of magnetism. In 1820, Oersted showed current carrying wires produced magnetic fields.

Chapter 2

UNIFIED PHYSICS

Planck presented his quantum theory of energy in 1900. It was partly formed because of his search to provide a thermodynamic interpretation of the radiation law. Planck figured light, electromagnet waves, and radiation curved when heated, and could not be given off at a set rate; therefore, he determined that emissions and absorption were given off in packets that he called quanta. Later, Planck's quanta were called photon. The quantum theory changed research on atomic structure from the kinetic theory of gases.

Rutherford and Soddy in 1903 laid a foundation for radioactivity, and in 1905 published their findings. Rutherford and Geiger invented the Geiger counter two years later.

In 1905 Einstein published four papers in the German journal *Annalen der Physik (Annals of Physics)*. These four papers remarkably changed Physics. In the first of the four papers, Einstein presented a formula for displacement of particles in suspension. It was the second of the four papers that Einstein won the Nobel Price for Physics in 1921 on the electromagnetic radiation and photoelectric effect. In the third of the four papers Einstein introduced his special theory of relativity, and in the fourth of the four papers presented $E=mc^2$. This is often referred to as Einstein's "annus mirabilis" or miracle year.

Einstein's special theory of relativity of 1905 changed electromagnetic concepts from mechanical concepts to fundamental concepts; and declared ether as unnecessary. Einstein's light quantum hypothesis of 1905 used light as a

7

particulate. Also Einstein noted the equivalence of mass and energy, and united these categories providing a framework for a unified physics. Einstein, in the fourth of his 1905 papers proposed energy equals mass times the speed of light squared ($E=mc^2$). The equation's simplicity is basic and vast in that it includes everything.

Dirac added the plus/minus to Einstein's equation of $E=mc^2$ because it was needed to make it mathematically correct making it $E=\pm mc^2$. Einstein appreciated Dirac's addition to the formula to express it correct mathematically and called it the Dirac-Einstein equation.

In 1907, Minkowski developed the mathematics that improved Einstein's special theory of relativity. When Einstein published his special theory of relativity in 1905, he used Euclidean three-dimensional geometry. Minkowski knew he could unify Einstein's concepts of space and time, energy and matter, as well as electricity and magnetism, by using the fourth dimension. Einstein realized that Minkowski's suggestion was an improvement, and Einstein used it; and also used it in his general theory of relativity in 1916 in the curvature of space-time and gravitation. Minkowski, using fourth dimension mathematics, consolidated Maxwell's eight partial equations to two equations which was an improvement in describing light.

In working with energy-mass and space-time, Einstein changed all points, particles, energies, masses, and solid bodies, utilizing them as fields. Thus fields became Faraday and Einstein's contribution to any unified field theory. Einstein emphasized motion occurring within energy-mass and space-time. He also realized gravity was involved in the warping of space-time.

Leavitt (1908) discovered that. a group of stars called Cepheid had a consistent variation in brightness that was regular. Astronomers used this to calculate distances of galaxies up to ten million light years away. In 1912, Leavitt improved his method of calculating the distances, and it is still being used today.

Einstein extended Planck's quantum work to include a theory on light. Einstein gave a lecture in 1909 that light could have both particle and wave like properties. Einstein wrote several papers explaining and supporting the quantum theory.

In 1909, Einstein's equivalency principle basically stated that gravitational mass and inertial mass are equivalent, and also gravity and acceleration are equivalent. The equivalency principle also indicated the path of light rays would be affected by a gravitational field. Einstein determined the size of an atom by mathematical calculations.

In 1911, Rutherford published that the atom had a nucleus with a positive charge surrounded by electrons with a negative charge which balanced the atom.

Einstein knew that light traveled in straight lines, but that light would be deflected by any object with mass which was in its path. In 1911, Einstein predicted the starlight just grazing the sun in a total eclipse would be deflected, and made his mathematical calculations.

Eddington went from England to an island off the west coast of Africa to view the total eclipse of the sun on May 29, 1919, that he observed and recorded. He found his measurements matched Einstein's 1911 calculations of the very slight bending of light by the gravitational field of the sun. This was the first of many confirmations that proved Einstein's theory was correct; and that the universe was viewed as predicted in his general theory of relativity. It was partly through Eddington's work that Einstein's general theory of relativity was translated from German into the English language.

Einstein and Grossmann decided to check Einstein's theory and mathematics to determine if it was accurate by figuring Mercury's perihelion. It was calculated with only a 43 seconds difference. Later while completing his 1916 paper on general relativity, Einstein recalculated his computations on the basis of his theory and accounted for the 43 seconds.

In November of 1915, Einstein presented three separate papers to the Prussian Academy in Berlin; and then published them as one theory in 1916 in the *Annuals of Physics* as the *Foundations of the General Theory of Relativity*. This was the first edition of Einstein's complete general theory of relativity.

In 1920, Heisenberg developed matrices, an algebraic entity, for use in the quantum theory. Physicists liked and used Schrodinger's quantum mathematics based on calculus which was easier to use than the matrices.

In 1920, Szilard came to study under Einstein who was impressed how Szilard handled the problem of utilizing thermodynamics to fluctuating systems. Einstein and Szilard worked together filing numerous patent applications in Europe. Their collaboration ended after seven years when the Nazis came to power, and Szilard decided to leave Germany.

In 1921, Bose became interested in Planck's study of radiation. Bose wrote a paper using a new approach by placing photons on an energy level to obtain Planck's formula using quantum concepts. Bose's paper was rejected for publication. Bose sent his paper to Einstein for suggestions. Einstein made a number of corrections to Bose's paper, and then realized that Bose's work on photons could also be applied to atoms and molecules. Einstein saw it as a new form of statistics distinct from Bolzmann's statistics. Einstein called the new method Bose-Einstein statistics, and published the paper in 1924. Two weeks later, Einstein submitted a second paper showing that the Bose-Einstein statistics could be used as a quantum statistic for radiation.

Einstein used the Bose-Einstein statistics to look at gases at low temperatures and realized atoms would loose their viscosity. Keeson and Leydon confirmed this in 1928; but Einstein calculated properties of atoms all the way down to absolute zero. Einstein realized that cooled to near zero the quantum wave packets of atoms would compact into a single macroscopic wave packet, and form a new matter which he called superatoms using the Bose-Einstein condensate. Scientists were slow to accept Einstein's work because at that time there was no way of cooling to absolute zero.

The Bose-Einstein condensate was tested in 1985 when laser light was found to cool atoms. The Bose-Einstein condensate was utilized in 1995 and in 1997 in laser beams which turned the condensate atoms into synchronized lasers. In a laser beam all the photons are of the same frequency and in one phase so the laser beam can be controlled.

Friedmann, in 1922, noted that the universe looked identical in every direction and from any place; and discovered waves coming from all directions that were later called background radiation. Friedmann in 1922 and Lemaitre in 1927 had their own models of the universe, and were independently correct in their observations that the galaxies were moving away from each other,

De Broglie, influenced by Einstein's work, stated in his doctoral thesis in 1924 that matter could have both particle and wave like properties, and any mass in motion was a wave. The experimental support was done independently by Thompson and by Davisson. The wave like behavior of particles was used by Schrodinger in his formulation of wave mechanics. De Broglie was awarded the Nobel Prize in Physics in 1929.

In 1925, Heisenberg, Schrodinger, and Dirac reformulated the quantum hypothesis into quantum mechanics based on Heisenberg's uncertainty principle in which there are no definite results only possibilities and no specific results from a single measurement, but has a quantum state which is a combination of position and velocity. Many scientists liked and used the new quantum mechanistic theory as it was helpful in their research, and proved to be accepted and successful in nanotechnology, electronics, and other fields.

Einstein contributed extensively to the quantum theory at its beginning. With quantum mechanics based on chance and probability, particles no longer had separate well-defined positions and velocities that could be observed. In 1926, Einstein was questioning it as in the classical theory everything could be predicted, measured and weighed exactly. Einstein preferred classical physics, but continued to use the quantum hypothesis and the quantum mechanistic theory.

In 1927, Thompson and Davisson, working independently, provided evidence of the wave particle duality of the electron. Results were obtained in the same year therefore both shared a Nobel Prize in Physics in 1937 for discovery of the diffraction of electrons by crystals which provided evidence of the wave particle duality of the electron. The results were in agreement with de Broglie's equation for the electron's wavelength.

Schrodinger's wave equations were first tried to measure slow moving electrons compared to light. Then he measured the motion of atoms, electrons, and waves using the quantum mechanistic theory of probability of position and velocity. In 1928, Schrodinger's equations became basic to quantum mechanics. He shared a Nobel Prize in Physics in 1933 with Dirac.

In 1928, Dirac's theory explained the electron by using both quantum mechanics and Einstein's special theory of relativity. Dirac also predicted the electron would have an anti-electron. The discovery of the positron in 1932 confirmed Dirac's theory. In 1933, Dirac shared a Nobel Prize in Physics with Schrodinger.

Jeans (1928) observed newly formed matter erupting from the cores of galaxies. He studied the spiral arms of the galaxies (later called nebula) that were formed and remained intact despite all the motion within them. Jeans figured how to calculate the amount of radiation that a galaxy or star radiated.

Chandrasekhar (Chandra) figured solar solutions to stellar star collapses in 1930. He calculated that a cold star of one and a half times the sun would not be able to support itself against its own gravity, and this is known as the Chandrasekhar limit. A super star can throw off enough material to reduce itself to a stable size. It is the thermal energy plus radiation flowing out from the core of an active star that keeps it from collapsing under its own weight. Chandrasekhar shared the Nobel Prize in Physics in 1983.

Hubble (1930) published his results that the galaxies were moving away and the universe was expanding, which was proposed earlier in the 1920s by both Friedmann and Lemaitre. Hubble figured how to estimate the distances of galaxies, and used the Doppler's effect to judge their speed. The Hubble's constant is a ratio of two numbers, the recessional velocity of a galaxy divided by its distance, and it is one of the most important constants in cosmology. The mathematics Hubble used solving his constant was complicated, but Refsdal when working out the mathematics for Einstein's theory of gravitational lenses found he could apply it to Hubble's constant to calculate it directly with only a slightly lower difference in time.

Originally, Einstein when writing his general theory of relativity formulated the cosmological constant. With confirmation by Hubble, Friedmann, Lemaitre, and others that the universe was expanding and changing, Einstein stated the cosmological constant was his mistake, and Einstein withdrew his constant from his theory in writing in 1931. Since 1998, cosmologists, making observations of supernovas, are using Einstein's cosmological constant as a vital tool in their work, and also using it involving the universe's expansion.

In 1933, Einstein, Podolsky, and Rosen (EPR) presented an experimental challenge to quantum physicists. At first, there was no satisfactory conclusion. To help the situation, Bell set up and monitored a challenge. A dozen scientists responded to the challenge, and it was Aspect's experiment that proved quantum mechanics was correct, and it was verified by other scientists each working independently. Quantum mechanics is a theory of the very small, and has been successful in numerous applications.

Fermi published the first Italian text on modern physics in 1928 in an effort to modernize physics in Italy. Before his departure from Rome, he made advances in theoretical and experimental fields. He worked to advance Irene and Frederick Joliot-Cure in 1934 in their production of artificial radioactive isotopes.

In 1934, Fermi's experiments showed neutrons projected into a nucleus created new and heavier nuclei, but he did not analyze the results. Hahn and Strassmann's experiments with uranium showed the nucleus would split in two, and published the results. Hahn wrote to Meitner for her opinion and she did the mathematics which showed the reaction was correct. She told her nephew, Frisch, a physicist, who called the process fission. When Frisch returned to Copenhagen, he explained the results to Bohr, but the news was spread by an assistant. The news reached Fermi who realized a chain reaction could occur. Szilard conceived of a chain reaction several years earlier, and had taken out a patent on the process. Szilard contacted Einstein and they wrote a letter to President Roosevelt. When only minor action resulted, Szilard went to Einstein to write another letter to Roosevelt that the Germans had a project using uranium and believed they were building a bomb. England sent a concerned report to the United States. In 1942, Fermi was given permission to test a chain reaction that showed a bomb could be built, and Oppenheimer was put in charge. In Germany, the Nazis put Heisenberg in charge to build a nuclear reactor in 1940. Because the Norwegian underground destroyed the heavy water the Germans needed for their reactor, the work on the German bomb was never completed. The United States built and used the atomic bomb. Later, in the construction of the hydrogen bomb, the complicated process for the conversion of hydrogen to helium called fusion was calculated by Bethe. The hydrogen bomb was built, tested, but never used.

Meitner received the Fermi Prize from the Atomic Energy Commission. The International Union of Pure and Applied Chemistry approve the name of meiterium for the element 109 in honor of Meitner, element Einsteinium (99) for Einstein, element fermium (100) for Fermi, and element Lawrencium (103) for Lawrence. Nobel Prizes in Physics were awarded to Fermi in 1938, to Lawrence in 1939, and to Bethe in 1967; and Hahn received a Nobel Prize in Chemistry in 1944.

In 1935, Einstein and Rosen experimented with the principles of quantum atomic particles and the principles of electricity between two flat surfaces of space-time geometry called Einstein and Rosen Bridges. The particles traveling from one surface to the other surface reacted to gravity and curvature, then to closure and opening. The quantum theory was able to account for the atomic and quantum phenomena, but the principles of relativity did not. The Einstein-Rosen bridge concept is now utilized as wormholes connecting two universes, and shortcuts through space-time.

In 1945, Feynman began to consider some of the problems in quantum electrodynamics dealing with interactions between electrons and photons. In 1948, Feynman's approach was sum over histories method (motion of path integrals), and in 1949 he showed how to calculate path integrals with Feynman's diagrams. He shared the 1965 Nobel Prize in Physics with Schwinger and Tomonaga.

In the fifth edition of Einstein's general theory of relativity, he simplified the field equations of the theory of gravity without changing its meaning by the addition of Appendix II in December of 1954. This he did partly with his assistant, Kaufman, to make it clearer without changing the theory.

An important discovery was made in 1964 by Penzias and Wilson of cosmic microwave background radiation, and beat Dicke and Peebles to the discovery and publication of the radiation. The cosmic background radiation was originally predicted by Friedman in 1922, Lemaitre in 1927, and by Gamow and Alpher in 1948. Penzias and Wilson received the Nobel Prize in Physics in 1978 with Kapitsa.

In 1968, Feynman solved the Stanford Linear Accelerator's nuclear interaction problem with a component he named partons that did not interact with each other.

Penrose and Hawking proved a theorem of Einstein's general theory relativity that a collapsing star would form a singularity and they published it in 1970. Hawking realized by reversing time in their theory, he could show the big bang originated the universe from a singularity. Einstein's mathematics agreed with Lemaitre's primeval atom that would explode outward with a big bang. Hoyle and others said the temperature was too even to allow the galaxies to evolve from it. Supporters of the big bang theory worked to find slight variations in temperature that would allow for the formation of galaxies in the cosmic background radiation. Smoot and team, to prove Hawking's reversal of the theory was correct, obtained a place from NASA for the Cosmic Background Explorer (COBE) that was launched in a rocket in 1989. The information obtained was abundant and confirmed Penzias and Wilson's 1964 background radiation was from the big bang. In 1992, computer generated maps of the early universe from COBE's data revealed tiny temperature variations in the cosmic background radiation allowing galaxies to form and evolve in the universe. They confirmed the big bang theory.

Rubin (1983) realized the rotation of the spiral galaxies were affecting each other gravitationally, and thought they should rotate together. Rubin measured the velocities of the spirals using the Doppler shift. She reported there had to be something not visible that was holding the stars in position. It was later acknowledged and labeled dark matter.

In 1985, Chu, Cohen-Tannoudje, and Phillips showed that laser light could be used to cool atoms to a millionth of a degree above absolute zero for a half second, for which they shared the 1997 Nobel Prize in Physics.

Cornell and Weiman worked from 1989 to 1995 to complete their own apparatus to observe the Bose-Einstein condensate, and took a photo using laser light. They produced a Bose-Einstein condensate of twenty billionths of a degree above absolute zero.

Ketterle, using a Bose-Einstein condensate, produced an atomic laser by first cooling the atoms to condense them, and then irradiating them into a synchronized beam. Cornell, Weiman, and Ketterle shared the Nobel Prize in Physics in 2001.

These are only some of the highlights of the work accomplished by those in physics and the related sciences. As we look at the progress made, it gives us an appreciation of their challenges, endeavors, and successes. The world is appreciative of their accomplishments.

Chapter 3

THE SPECTROSCOPE

The passage of light through a prism is separated into a spectrum. When light from the sun or from a bright lamp is shown through an ordinary prism, we see a band of colors. The colors of the spectrum of the sun light are red, orange, yellow, green, blue, indigo, and violet. The ultra-violet spectrum is at the end of the violet spectrum. The separation of colors is called dispersion. The longest wavelengths are red, and the shortest wavelengths are violet.

There are three types of spectra: absorption, continuous, and bright-line spectra. Absorption spectra are the most numerous. Continuous emission spectra are important as their waves are shorter than visible light; and they can be detected by fluorescent and photoelectric effects, and quartz mercury lamps. The bright-line spectra is used to give every element a particular pattern of bright spectra lines for identification, and will show what percentage of a substance is present.

The wave length emitted by a particular atom is the same wherever that atom is in the universe. Electromagnetic data can be obtained from every atom in the universe by spectral analyses. The study of spectra has helped in chemical analysis, and in determining the structure of atoms and molecules.

Infrared radiations are shown as spectra's long waves beyond the red boundary with strength dependent on the temperature of the item. A continual exchange of radiation is going on as energy is given or received.

Newton discovered when light passed through a prism it displayed colors as in a rainbow. Then Newton produced the same display directly from a telescope, and there was an overlapping of colors. Newton eliminated this by directing the beam of light through a slit to a lens to throw the image onto a screen which showed the colors with no overlapping.

Von Fraunhofer (1814) did not immediately understand the significance of his observation of the spectra of light through his lamp lens. He called them Fraunhofer lines, and they are an indication of the chemical composition of the solar atmosphere.

In 1860, Kirchhoff and Bunsen proved each chemical element when heated has light, and furnishes a bright-line spectrum giving the percentage of a substance that is present. Bunsen developed the Bunsen burner in 1855 which is used in laboratories similar to the one used by Faraday.

Huggins discovered that the sun and the stars were similar as he used the spectroscope showing hydrogen and helium giving off heat and light. In 1863, Huggins concluded that the colors in the spectrum showed the elements present in the source of light.

Aston (1919) improved the design of the spectrograph by using a magnetic field. Aston received the Nobel Price for Chemistry in 1922 for the design and use of his new spectrograph. Aston then improved his spectrograph for use on solids, and to show atomic weights.

Astronomers looking at the spectra of stars observed if a star was moving away, the lines shift toward the red end of the spectrum (red shift), and if the star was approaching, the lines shift toward the blue end of the spectrum (blue shift).

Chapter 4

THE PERIODIC TABLE AND ISOTOPES

PERIODIC TABLE OF THE ELEMENTS

Atoms differ greatly in weight, chemical properties, ability to combine, and in stability.

Dalton wrote the first atomic theory of matter in 1802; and assigned mass to atoms of the elements by assuming hydrogen had a mass of one. Later, carbon was assigned as the standard, and elements were assigned atomic masses.

The periodic table was designed by Mendelyee in 1869 at a time when only 63 elements were known. When new elements were discovered they fit neatly into the spaces he reserved for them. Mendelyee noted gold and tellurium atomic weights were possibly incorrect, and soon they were corrected. He noted three open spaces in his table were probably similar elements, and listed their physical properties which helped in their discovery.

Mendelyee arranged the periodic table of elements by the atom's mass which increases steadily as read from left to right, and in vertical columns, the atoms are chemically similar which gives orderly atomic mass and atomic numbers.

In 1913, Moseley designed the periodic table that we use today with each element's block showing the name, symbol, atomic number, and atomic mass; and is placed by atomic number very similar to Mendelyee's arrangement. Besides identification, the table is useful to help in the combination of elements into chemical compounds.

Hydrogen is the most abundant element in the solar system with ninety-one percent, and helium second with nine percent. The percentage of elements of the earth is different than those in the solar system. The percent of elements comprising the living organisms are basically hydrogen sixty-three, oxygen twenty-five, carbon nine, and nitrogen one percent. The percent of elements of the human body's mass are oxygen sixty-five, carbon eighteen, hydrogen ten, and nitrogen three percent. The percentages of elements not listed are relatively small that make up the total.

In 1940, uranium was bombarded with neutrons and produced neptunium, the heaviest known atom at the time. The University of California Berkeley group found four elements still higher in atomic number: americium, curium, berkelium and californium, which fit into the periodic table.

Presently there are 109 distinct elements, with only 90 elements found naturally and the others are made in the laboratory or with atomic accelerators and nuclear reactors.

ISOTOPES

The element and all the isotopes of an element go by the same name and symbol; all have the same nuclear charge, all have the same number of electrons per atom, all have the same atomic number, and all have the same chemical properties, but not the same atomic mass. The nuclei in isotopes contain uncharged particles called neutrons that act as a ballast for the difference in mass. Three-fourths of the elements have two or more isotopes. Atomic mass refers to the mass whole number of an element. An isotope's mass number is the whole number nearest to the atomic mass number of its element.

Thompson, (1910) working with the original mass spectrograph discovered some elements with the same name, the same symbol, the same place on the periodic table, the same nuclear charge, the same number of electrons per atom, the same atomic number, and the same chemical properties, but they did not have the same atomic mass. These were soon called isotopes. About three fourths of the elements occur in two or more isotopic forms.

Soddy introduced the idea of isotopes in 1913. The term isotope came from the study of radioactive elements formed in the process of radioactive disintegration. Soddy was awarded the Nobel Prize in Chemistry in 1921 for his study on isotopes and radioactive substances.

Aston, with the new precise mass spectrometer he developed, found isotopes are not restricted to radioactive elements but are throughout the elements. Aston was awarded the Nobel Prize in Chemistry in 1922 for classifying isotopes using the mass spectrograph and perfecting the whole number rule of the structure and weight of atoms.

Artificial radioactivity was discovered by Irene and Frederic Joliot-Curie in 1933, and they received the 1935 Nobel Prize in Chemistry for synthesizing new radioactive elements.

Segre produced many new radioactive isotopes by bombarding uranium with neutron.

Chapter 5

MICROSCOPES, THE SCANNING TUNNELING MICROSCOPE, AND MICROSCOPY

In a compound or refracting microscope with two convex lenses, an object is placed close to the lower lens which produces a real image between the second lens (eye piece) and its focal point. The eye piece produces a magnified image of the real image.

In an optical microscope, the resolution is limited by the wavelength of the waves used to make the image, and has a resolution of 2000 Å, about half the wavelength of visible light.

An electron microscope (EM) has a 2 Å resolution by using electron waves. The electron momentum is two percent of the speed of light. The electron microscope uses magnetic fields for both its objective and projection lenses with an electromagnet or a permanent magnet. A beam of electrons focused on a thin slice of sample is controlled by electrostatic or magnetic deflection which acts on the charges focusing the beam into an image on a fluorescent screen for examination or on a photographic plate for photographing. A diffusion pump provides the vacuum.

A scanning tunneling microscope (STM) has a lateral resolution of about 2 Å, and a vertical resolution of 0.01 Å. A scan with the tip of the probe can reach the atomic level, or one one-hundredth of an atom's diameter, when mounted on a piezoelectric scanner. A scanning tunneling microscope measures the electrical force conductivity between a tip and the sample rather than an electrical current when viewing metals.

In the scanning tunneling microscope, a platinum radium needle scans across the sample. The needle is attached to a cylinder of piezoelectric current that expands and contracts lengthwise in response to the electric current. When the tip of the needle is brought very close to the surface, the electrons tunnel across the space and modify the potential difference.

Tunneling is a quantum mechanical technique of transferring of electrons from one piece of metal to another piece of metal a few Å apart so the electrons can flow across. The beginning work on tunneling was done by Giaever and Esaki who received the Nobel Prize in Physics in 1973 with Josephson.

Rohrer and Binning improved the tunneling idea, and invented the scanning tunneling microscope in 1980 that measures the electrical conductivity force between the tip and the surface. Rohrer and Binning received a Nobel Prize in Physics in 1986 for their invention of the scanning tunneling microscope, and shared it with Ruska for his invention of the electron microscope. Binning developed a similar force scanning tunneling microscope for biology.

The atomic force microscope (AFM) measures the force between the tip and sample rather than direct current which uses the quantum exclusion principle depending on the tip sample separation, same as the scanning tunneling microscope. The atomic force tunneling microscope measures the force between the tip and the sample. The atomic force microscope is used for technological applications, especially detailed and precise descriptions of a place or region.

Molecular beam techniques (MBT) are being used, and one advantage is that specific crystal planes can be looked at by directing a beam on an oriented surface with known steps and densities. Another advantage is the length of time a particle may be on the surface to be measured.

In field emission microscopy (FEM), the sample is in the form of a filament etched to a sharp tip and enclosed within a chamber fitted with a fluorescent screen. When a potential difference is applied between the sample and the screen, electrons give a flash of light when they strike the screen. The ease with which the electrons can escape from the metal depends on the experiment.

The field ionization microscopy (FIM) is the same as the FEM except the potential difference is reversed with the fluorescent screen made negative to the tip. In the experiment, a small quantity of helium is admitted which migrates across the surface until it is ionized at an exposed atom.

Atom-probe field ionization microscopy (AP-FIM) is used in surgery. Basically, the location of the atom and where it is in the sample can be observed, shown on a screen, with a mass spectrometer behind the screen so the atom can be identified.

Chapter 6

FIELD FOUNDATIONS AND FUNDAMENTAL FORCES OF THE UNIVERSE

FIELD FOUNDATIONS

FRANKLIN'S STUDY OF ELECTRICITY

Franklin, in 1750, established that electricity travels in one direction from its source (positive) to its negative termination. Franklin introduced the terms positive and negative as he referred them to electricity; and he contributed to the understanding of grounding and insulation. Franklin proved that lightning and electricity were the same.

Franklin designed the first lightning rods for structures to direct lightning away from buildings into the ground. As the concepts of fields developed, investigations were applied to practical inventions including many by Franklin.

OERSTED AND AMPERE'S CURRENTS AND FIELDS

In 1820, Oersted discovered electric currents produced magnet fields. Influenced by Oersted's work, Ampere was credited with developing a mathematical theory of the relationships between electric currents and magnetic fields in 1825.

FARADAY'S FORCE FIELDS

Faraday placed iron filings on a sheet of paper over a magnet to show the filings formed a visible pattern called force fields. The iron filings indicate where the fields of force are located as they are invisible. When two magnets of opposite charges (+/- or -/+) are used, the iron filling go from one magnetic pole to the other magnetic pole, at the speed of light, which displays attraction. When two magnets with like charges (+/+ or -/-) are used, the iron filings do not travel from magnetic pole to magnetic pole but are repelled as the force field of the filings are sent back to their original poles. These force field examples are illustrated in class rooms and text books as an experimental foundation of fields.

Faraday discovered the basic nature of magnetism and electricity. In 1820, Faraday worked with magnetic fields and electric currents to induce an electric current by magnetic action. In 1831 he published the results of his work in *Experimental Researches in Electricity.*

MAXWELL'S ELECTROMAGNETIC FIELD AND ELECTROMAGNETIC FORCE

In 1860, Maxwell, based on Faraday work, succeeded in unifying the partial theories of electricity and magnetism, and those by Cavendish and Coulomb. Maxwell showed mathematically that a single field carries electricity and the magnetic force. Maxwell proved they are an inseparable force which he called the electromagnetic force, and the field that carries the electromagnetic force is the electromagnetic field.

Maxwell, when developing the theory of electromagnetism, explained the known effects of magnetism. Faraday showed a changing magnetic field induced an electric current in a wire, and Maxwell showed that the opposite is also true, a changing electric field induces a magnetic field. Maxwell described electricity and magnetism in four mathematical equations which showed they travel through space in the form of waves at the speed of light by electric and magnetic fields. Hertz verified Maxwell's mathematics by producing electromagnetic waves in the laboratory.

In 1860, Maxwell paid a personal tribute to Faraday that he (Maxwell) could never have done the mathematics if it were not for Faraday's excellent descriptions of force fields.

EINSTEIN'S FIELD CONCEPTS

Einstein's contribution to fields was using Faraday's concept of fields by changing and utilizing all particles and materialistic points as fields.

Einstein utilized electromagnetic fields as presented by Maxwell, and calculated that light waves are electromagnetic field waves. The electromagnetic field can be shielded, but nothing stops the gravitational field.

Einstein's special theory of relativity of 1905 can be conceived as a field theory. Einstein's unification concepts of the field theory led to his study of energy-mass fields, and an expanded view of the atom.

FEYNMAN'S FIELD CHANGES IN CHARGE AND DIRECTION OF MOTION

In 1945, Feynman discovered an electromagnetic field would automatically change its charge when its direction changes. All mass fields are bound to their direction of motion as long as the element does not change its motion to an ellipse, and when a mass field does change its motion, it becomes an anti-mass field.

THE FOUR FUNDAMENTAL PHYSICAL FORCES OF THE UNIVERSE

Scientists and mathematicians recognize four fundamental physical forces within the universe: electromagnetic force, strong nuclear force, weak nuclear force and gravitational force. All particles are subject to these four forces which are defined by their strength.

The interaction of particles within the four forces is described as force field particles: in the electromagnetic force they are photons, in the strong nuclear force they are gluons, in the weak nuclear force they are bosoms, and in the gravitational force they are gravitons. The force field particles are interactions or mediations between particles.

ELECTROMAGNETIC FORCE

The electromagnetic force is a long-range force with a range throughout the universe, infinite, and stronger than the gravitational force.

The electromagnetic force interacts with positive and negative electrical charged particles. Electric forces exist between stationary charged particles, and magnetic forces exist between moving charged particles. The electromagnetic force interacts with electrically charged positive and negative particles. The long-range effects of the electromagnetic force are not observed because there is usually a negative electric charge for every positive electric charge, and a south magnetic pole for every north magnetic pole with the effects of electromagnetism canceling out. On a large scale, such as the sun and the earth, the attraction and repulsion charges cancel and there is little electromagnetic force activity.

The electromagnetic force is extremely active within atoms and molecules, and is responsible for binding them. The electromagnetic force holds electrons in orbit around the nuclei in atoms.

Interaction of force field particles in the electromagnetic force is mediated by photons.

The foundation of electromagnetism is used in lasers, televisions, computers, internet, and other electronic and magnetic phenomena.

STRONG NUCLEAR FORCE

The strong nuclear force has a microscopic range within the nucleus. The strong nuclear force holds the nucleus of an atom together which has large electric forces of repulsion between particles. It binds the protons and neutrons in the nuclei. The strong nuclear force is the strongest of the four forces.

Matter on earth is made up mainly of protons and neutrons that are broken down into fundamental particles called quarks. The strong nuclear force holds the quarks together in the protons and neutrons, and holds the protons and neurons together in the nucleus of the atom. The strong nuclear force is stronger than the electromagnetic forces inside the nuclei.

The interaction of force field particles in the strong nuclear force is mediated by gluons.

The strong nuclear force has a confinement ability that binds particles together into combinations such as baryons and mesons that are made of quarks bound together by the strong force. Quarks can form stable particles called baryons of which protons and neutrons are examples. Anti-quarks can form anti-particles of the baryons. When such particles collide, they can exchange quarks.

The strong nuclear force has asymptotic possibility which means that it binds the quarks when they are close together. Quarks cannot be seen in nature or in the laboratory, but they explain the behavior of protons, neutrons and other particles of matter. Asymptotic possibility makes the concept of quarks and gluons understandable.

The strong nuclear force is referred to as the color force as it works with quarks.

WEAK NUCLEAR FORCE

The weak nuclear force is a short range force that produces instability in particles of certain nuclei and is involved in their breaking apart. It is also responsible for most radioactive decay processes. The weak nuclear force is not as strong as the strong nuclear force.

The nucleus is composed of protons and neutrons that are composed of quarks. The strong nuclear force holds quarks together, while the weak nuclear force helps to change a quark from one variety to another variety in the decay process.

The interaction of force field particles in the weak nuclear force is mediated by bosoms.

Higgs in 1964 discovered a massive particle he called Higgs boson. The Higgs boson is a subatomic particle proposed as a force field particle acting on mass. Because of the difference in mass between the electromagnetic force and the weak nuclear force at low energies, Higgs bosom particles could provide a mechanism for breaking the electroweak symmetry. It is elusive as it disintegrates quickly.

Salam and Weinberg proposed unification of the weak nuclear force with the electromagnetic force. Glashow had suggested the same unification. In 1967, Salam and Weinberg unified weak effects on particles with the electromagnetic force just as Maxwell had unified electricity and magnetism 100 years earlier. The work found symmetry breaking of particles. Salam, Weinberg and Glashow received the Nobel Prize for physics in 1979 for unifying the electromagnetic force and weak nuclear force as the electroweak force.

Van der Meer and Rubbia successfully tested the unification of the electromagnet force and the weak nuclear force using the accelerator of the Large Hadron Collider's super proton synchrotron with the aid of a technique by van der Meer in 1972. Rubbia and van der Meer received a Nobel Prize in Physics for this work in 1984.

GRAVITATIONAL FORCE

The gravitational force is universal, infinite, and holds the universe together. Gravity is the attraction that exists between all masses, and it is the weakest of the four forces, but it has an unlimited range in the universe.

The gravitational force is the force that holds the planets, stars and galaxies together. Its effect on elementary particles is negligible.

The earth's gravitational force causes objects to move toward it, and the moon's gravitational force causes the earth's tides. Every particle is affected by gravity according to its mass and energy.

The interaction of force field particles in the gravitational force is mediated by gravitons. Gravitons are instrumental in forming gravitational waves, but they are very weak.

The gravitational force was proposed by Newton in 1678 explaining the orbital paths of planets around the sun. Ideas on gravity and gravitation were always of interest, and especially with Einstein's special theory of relativity (1905) and the general theory of relativity (1916).

About 1908, Einstein while studying gravity and formulating the general theory of relativity, correlated gravitation to the quantum theory. Einstein showed gravity affected the speed of light, stretches the waves of light, and bends their path.

It has been said Einstein's theory on gravity is the most informative ever written. Einstein also wrote an equation which proposed that gravity interacted with light photons.

In the 1980s most scientists began to apply the concepts of gravitation and space-time mathematically in their equations.

FORCE OF LIFE AND FORCE OF FAITH

The four fundamental forces of the universe pertain to the sciences. There are two other forces that pertain to everyone that some physicists, mathematicians, and engineers recognize, but seldom express.

FORCE OF LIFE

There is a force of life. As long as one has breath, one has this living force of life. It is with this living force that life is experienced and enjoyed, and that life can be improved and benefited. It is not what one can do, but what one does with this force of life. Einstein, on social problems, commented it was the duty of every man of good will to make the teaching of pure humanity a living force.

FORCE OF FAITH

There is another force, a force of faith. This faith force for some is their bases of hope, guidance and wisdom in their relationship with God, nature, their fellow man, and their conscience; and that each experience is personal, intimate, fulfilling and satisfying.

Chapter 7

THE EXPANDING UNIVERSE

The invisible expansion force that spreads the universe outward is believed to be the inflationary energy generated by the big bang. This expansion force is estimated to have been active for some fifteen billion years.

The expansion force acts like antigravity and exerts an outward force opposite to gravity. It is the inflationary energy at the time of the big bang that is self-generating and causing the expanding universe. Its speed has decreased since the big bang.

The universe's space is expanding taking the galaxies and stars with it. The expansion of the universe is only the expansion of the universe's space. As the universe expands, the amount of space between the widely separated galaxies and stars increases, but the size and number of the galaxies and stars remain the same. The universe is expanding between five and ten percent every billion years.

The countering force to expansion is gravity. The gravitational force of the universe counteracts the expansion's anti-gravity force so there a balance of forces.

The red shift caused by the expansion of the universe shown on a prism is properly called a cosmological red shift to distinguish it from the Doppler shifts. Doppler shifts are caused by an object's motion through space, whereas a cosmological red shift is caused by the expansion of space. For example: when a photon is traveling through expanding space, its wavelength becomes stretched, and the photon seen has a longer wavelength than usual shown by the cosmological red shift; and the longer the photon's journey, the more its wavelength will be stretched.

Therefore, photons from distant galaxies have larger red shifts than protons from nearby galaxies.

The Fraunhofer lines in refracted light are shifted toward the red in their light spectra. The speed at which an object travels in the expanding universe is progressively faster as the distance increases.

Hubble's law is the ratio of velocity and distance. The greater the distance to a galaxy, then the greater the galaxy's red shift. The rate of expansion can be determined by measuring the velocities that other galaxies are moving away from us using the Doppler effect. The galaxies farthest away in the expansion are traveling away faster than the closer galaxies.

Astronomers and cosmologists consider the expansion force is the explosive outward force generated by the big bang.

This energy was acknowledged in 1916 by Einstein using his cosmological constant to correct his mathematics as he counteracted the anti-gravity forces when he thought the universe was stable. When Einstein later realized the universe was not stable but expanding, he declared his cosmological constant was his big mistake; but most astronomers and cosmologists are now using it in their computations of the expansion of the universe.

Frenk built a database with information including facts on the rate of expansion, size, and mass of galaxies for a computer model of the expanding universe. He used equations from Einstein's general theory of relativity and information the way particles and energy are predicted to behave. Frenk can run his computer model of the universe backward and forward in time.

Faber and her colleagues have refined the techniques for analyzing the spectra from starlight. Faber and her team have developed a three dimensional computer image showing how the stars and galaxies are moving in relationship to each other. It basically shows the galaxies moving father away from each other as the space between them expands. They found a strong countercurrent of movement involving a large group of galaxies, including the Milky Way, moving at great speed toward another area. There are other strong currents involving other clusters and galaxies

Chapter 8

DARK ENERGY AND DARK MATTER

DARK ENERGY

Dark energy is known by observing visible matter. Although dark energy is invisible, the results of dark energy's activity can be seen, measured and calculated by using the velocities exhibited by galaxies and stars in motion in the universe. Dark energy is also known and referred to as energy density.

The source of dark energy has two main theories: In the inflation theory, Guth showed that if supercooling occurred in the early universe, a negative pressure would have been created to generate negative gravity resulting in an expansion with initial energy that is self-generating. In the other theory, Quantum electrodynamics discovered virtual particles in particle reactions that give off energy that are considered to be dark energy.

In 2004, Greene estimated the universe's total mass was counted as seventy percent to be dark energy and twenty-five percent to be dark matter and the balance of five percent to be visible matter or familiar matter that we know and see. Most scientists calculate the percentages approximately the same.

DARK MATTER

Dark matter is invisible, and is called dark because there is no radiation, heat or light coming from it, and it does not show up on photographs. Dark matter is known because of its gravitational attraction on the orbiting stars in the galaxies, and in gravitational lensing. It is dense, and it has so much mass that it can hold stars and galaxies in position. Dark matter makes its presence known through its gravitational field. Dark matter is different from the ordinary matter of protons and neutrons.

Einstein's 1911 theory explained when a star or dark matter passes in front of a star, it distorts light from that star as we view it making it appears brighter. This technique is known as Einstein's gravitational lensing. This lensing effect is used in assisting astronomers to understand the universe, and to identify dark matter.

Most galaxies are in clusters with the presence of dark matter known by its gravitational effect on the motion of the galaxies. Visible evidence for massive dark matter is the extended halos coming from the rotation curves of the galaxies. A cluster of galaxies are held together by gravity, but additional dark matter mass has been observed in the center of the cluster to keep the galaxies bound in orbit. The dark matter needed to bind a cluster is estimated to be ten times greater than the mass of the galaxies.

In 1919, Einstein did a mathematical experiment to see if the mass of the sun could deflect the light from a star as the sun passed between the star and the earth during a total eclipse of the sun by the moon. Eddington took a photograph during the eclipse of the sun by the moon showing all the stars were in their normal positions except the one that was being studied. It was exactly where Einstein said it would be as the sun had a gravitational effect on the star, and it appeared to be in a different position. This proved that Einstein's theory of gravity was correct; and that light is bent by mass when its path is crossed. Eddington also discovered that the luminosity of a star is related to its mass.

Eddington's experiment lead a group of astrophysicists to form Massive Astrophysical Compact Halo Objects (MACHOs) to study and understand the dark matter in the movement of galaxies. They decided to use Einstein's gravitation lensing in the region of the Large Magellanic Cloud with a good halo which had an abundance of dark matter. This would produce good evidence of dark matter as a number of stars appeared to shine more brightly as the dark matter passed in front of some of the stars. The study by the MACHOs showed how dense the dark matter is and that it has a strong gravitational effect. The MACHOs were successful, but a long way from determining how much dark matter is in the universe, how much matter accounts for the rotational movement of galaxies, and how strong a gravitational effect it has.

In 1930, Oort estimated the mass of our galaxy by the gravitational pull on stars that were on the edge of the galaxy. He determined only about fifty percent of the mass of our galaxy was seen.

In 1931, Zwicky realized clusters of galaxies had to have several hundred times their mass to stay in place.

In 1972, Ostriker and Peebles showed spiral galaxies and the Milky Way would be unstable unless surrounded by an invisible halo of dark matter.

Rotation of the galaxies was the subject of Rubin's lecture in 1983. She was studying visible matter in the rotating spinning galaxies when she found mass missing. After re-checking, she continued to find the same results in her work. The missing mass was not radiating strong on any wavelength. Rubin's missing mass is what we now call dark matter and her findings were confirmed.

It is estimated dark matter constitutes ninety percent of the cluster's mass, and is distributed much like the visible matter in clusters.

Chapter 9

THE ATOM

The atom has a nucleus consisting of protons (positive charge) and neutrons (no charge). The nucleus is surrounded by negatively charged electrons that orbit the nucleus. The electric charges within the atom balance out and it is neutral. The strong nuclear force holds the nucleus together, and the electromagnetic force holds the atom together.

The positive nucleus contains the energy-mass of the atom. The proton has far more mass than an electron; and the nucleus contains uncharged particles (neutrons) in addition to its protons. The neutrons help hold the nucleus together. The number of protons in a complete atom is the atomic number of the element. All electrons are negatively charged. Electrons may be ejected from any atom by heat or bombardment, including light or x-rays. The positive protons can attract negatively charged electrons.

Loosely bound electrons in the orbits are farthest from the nucleus, and the tightly bound electrons in the orbits are closer to the nucleus. The atom cannot emit light or radiate energy unless at least one electron moves or jumps outward into another orbit. The electron orbits are called shells. Hydrogen has one electron but many orbit shells. Hydrogen is neutral when the nucleus bears just enough positive charge to balance one electron. The hydrogen's electron contributes little to the total mass of the atom.

All atoms are fundamentally based on the concept of charge interactions; and the electromagnetic force in each atom holds the atom together, and the particles exchanged are photons. The nucleus is the control center of the entire atom, and is held together by the strong nuclear force.

Atoms often combine to form molecules, and are held together by short-range forces of the strong nuclear force because of the atoms' electrical charge. When they exist in a solid state, they form geometrical patterns which sometimes show up as crystals.

A passing electron can push an electron away form its nucleus by electrical repulsion. A neutron is uncharged and is able to travel through solid matter. A neutron may be deflected or even stopped by a collision with a nucleus. A neutron is about one tenth of one percent greater than the proton's mass.

The nucleus' building block is the nucleon composed of fundamental particles called quarks. When the nucleon is electrically charged, it is a positive proton; and when the nucleon is electrically neutral, it is a neutral neutron.

Prout's 1815 hypothesis was that each atom's weight should be a whole number multiple of the hydrogen's weight. His hypothesis was forgotten until the twentieth century.

Almost a century later in 1896, Roentgen added to the beginning knowledge of the structure of the atom., Becquerel revolutionized the whole concept of the atom, and within a few years it led to the current structure of the atom.

In 1910, Rutherford discovered the nucleus by using alpha particles. The nucleus has a positive charge equal to the charge of the electrons in its atom to make the whole structure neutral without gain or loss of energy. The hydrogen's nucleus has just enough positive charge to balance one electron. In 1911, Rutherford published his model of the atom, but did not use the term nuclear until 1912. The idea of the nuclear atom was developed by Bohr.

Wilson's (1911) cloud chamber showed tracts of electrons, protons, and atomic particles that leave a trail of ions as they pass through a gas. The cloud chamber was useful to study subatomic particles, and with the addition of a magnetic field, made different particles identifiable by their tracks. Wilson shared the 1927 Nobel Prize in Physics with Compton who, in 1923, proposed a quantum theory of scattering meaning the x-ray beam of photons collide with electrons and eject the photons from the atom scattering them with reduced kinetic energy.

In 1913, Bohr provided a theory that became known as Bohr's atom using the hydrogen atom with one electron. The atom theory presented by Bohr satisfied classical physics, Einstein's photon theory of light, and Planck's original quantum theory. Bohr's basic points in his theory were: the electron moves in circular orbits about the nucleus, the atom is stable when the electron is in orbit, and continues indefinitely without gain or loss of energy, the atom radiates energy when the electron moves from orbit to the next outer orbit, and the size of the electron's orbit is determined by the electron's angular momentum about the nucleus. The energy given off by the atom is carried by the electromagnetic particle, the photon, which agrees with Einstein's photoelectric effect theory.

Bohr assumed electrons moved between energy levels, but did not pursue it, so Einstein followed up on it showing two types of transitions were possible.

In 1913, Bohr, on the basis of the quantum data by Planck and data of spectral analyses, figured that electrons orbit the nuclei at specific distances within the atom. This is the classical Bohr atom. Bohr's model of hydrogen's electron orbiting the nucleus with no neutron supported the quantum mechanistic theory. It was soon used in microscopic work.

Sommerfield in 1916 modified Bohr's atomic model by proposing that electrons are in elliptical orbits.

Bohr used the hydrogen atom to understand the bright-line spectrum when hydrogen gas was emitting light in a process of giving away energy and shrinking the electron's orbit. The atom does not emit any light because it has no expendable energy. The electron in the hydrogen atom is in the innermost orbit within the atom at its least energy. The electron must shift to an outer orbit in order to absorb energy or take emission from an external source. When the electron jumps from one orbit to another orbit around the nucleus, it obtains one quantum of radiation (one photon). Light is emitted in quanta when hydrogen is stimulated. Bohr's success was in showing that the electron in the hydrogen atom was equipped to emit the spectral line that was observed in the hydrogen spectrum. Bohr received a Nobel Prize in Physics in 1922.

In 1928, Dirac was the first to publish a theory that was consistent with both quantum mechanic and Einstein's special theory of relativity. The electron theory gave a proper understanding of the electron, and explained it mathematically. Dirac predicted that the electron had an anti-electron or positron. It is now known that every particle has an anti-particle, and when they meet, will annihilate each other. The discovery of the positron in 1932 confirmed Dirac's theory. Dirac received the Nobel Prize in Physics in 1933.

Chadwick (1932) was the first to clearly identify the uncharged neutrons in the atom. The neutron has almost the same mass as the proton but no electrical charge. The neutron accounted for the atomic activity observed in the atom with the nucleus (positive charge) and the electron (negative charge). Chadwick was awarded the Nobel Prize in Physics in 1935.

In 1964, Gell-Mann and others discovered protons and neutrons are particles of the atom, but when protons were collided with other protons or electrons at high speeds in a particle collider, it indicated they were composed of smaller particles. There are at least six quarks (up, down, strange, charmed, bottom and top). A proton contains two up quarks and one down quark, and a neutron contains two down quarks and one up quark. Other particles can be made of the other quarks (strange, charmed, bottom and top), but they have greater mass and decay rapidly into protons and neutrons. Gell-Mann received a Nobel Prize in Physics in 1969 for classification of nuclear particles and their interactions.

Chapter 10

WAVES, RAYS, AND RADIATION

Light is called electromagnetic radiation that consists of perpendicular oscillating electric fields and magnetic fields, and possesses both particle and wave characteristics. The distance between two successive wave crests is called the wavelength of the light. The frequency of light is the number of wave crests passing a given point in one second. The shorter the wavelength then the higher the frequency as the frequency of light is related to its wavelength. The amount of energy radiated by an object depends on its temperature. The hotter the object is, the more energy it releases.

The only difference in light and electromagnetic waves is in their frequency and wavelengths. Electromagnetic waves are radiated by any current carrying an alternating current. Radiation generated electromagnetic waves exhibit interference, diffraction, reflection, refraction and polarization.

Electromagnetic waves travel at the speed of light, carry both energy and momentum that can be delivered to a surface, and are transverse. The ratio of the electric field to the magnetic field in an electromagnetic wave equals the speed of light. All forms of radiation are produced by oscillating electric fields and magnetic fields.

Newton advanced a theory in 1672 that light consisted of a stream of particles through a given medium. He used it to explain the reflection and refraction of light. The Newton theory was favored for almost two centuries.

Huygens developed a wave theory of light in 1670, and described it in his book in 1690 that light was in waves, and were transverse waves in an elastic medium. It was mainly ignored until experiments on interference and diffraction supported Huygens' theory.

In 1801, Young gave support to the wave theory by showing light beams can interfere with one another.

In the early 1800s, Herschel discovered infrared radiation in an experiment with a prism. When he held a thermometer just beyond the red end of the visible spectrum, the thermometer showed it was exposed to an invisible form of energy which Herschel called infrared radiation.

In 1865, Maxwell developed the electromagnetic theory of light. Electromagnetic waves or electromagnetic radiation are invisible radiation such as the long waves of infrared and radio waves, and the invisible radiation such as the short waves of ultraviolet light. Maxwell predicted that light was a form of high frequency electromagnetic radiation. Maxwell's theory was that electromagnet waves travel the same speed as light, and his mathematical theory showed electromagnet fields and magnetic fields can move as waves.

Maxwell stated a changing magnetic field produces a changing electric field and a changing electric field produces a changing magnetic field. Electric fields and magnetic fields are perpendicular to each other, and both fields are perpendicular to the direction of motion of the wave which is characteristic of transverse waves, therefore electromagnetic waves are transverse waves.

Hertz, in 1887, succeeded in producing electromagnetic radiation a few centimeters long in wavelengths known as radio waves. He showed that radio waves, like light waves, could be reflected, refracted and diffracted. Hertz's experimental evidence confirmed Maxwell's electromagnetic theory of light.

Roentgen discovered x-rays in 1895 and gave an accurate description of its properties. X-rays are invisible to the eye, travel at or near the speed of light, are not deflected by electric fields or magnetic fields, and do not consist of beams of charged particles. X-rays have proved to be a valuable tool in medicine. Roentgen was awarded the first Nobel Prize in Physics in 1901.

Becquerel when studying magnetism and crystals constructed an electrometer to measure small electric currents. He discovered natural radioactivity in 1896. Becquerel then looked for x-rays in fluorescence when some salts absorbed ultraviolet radiation. In 1899, he showed part of uranium could be deflected by a magnetic field and consisted of charged particles. He received a Nobel Prize in Physics in 1903 with Marie and Pierre Curie, who isolated trace amount of radioactive substances in 1898. Later Marie Curie discovered radium and polonium both of which were highly radioactive, and was awarded a Nobel Prize in Chemistry in 1911.

Rutherford, in 1899, working on radioactivity named two emissions as alpha and beta: the alpha had little penetrating power but produced considerable ionization while the beta possessed little ionizing power. In 1900, Rutherford discovered a third emission, gamma rays, which were not affected by magnetic fields, and gave off high-energy electromagnetic radiation. Alpha particles are spontaneously ejected from atoms of radium and some of the radioactive elements. Isotopes of all elements with atomic numbers above eighty-three are radioactive.

Rutherford's thee types of rays are classified according to the nature of their electric charge, and according to their ability to penetrate matter: alpha rays are positive, beta rays are negative, and gamma ray are uncharged. Rutherford received a Nobel Prize in Chemistry in 1908 for his work that atoms can be penetrated, and changed by alpha radiations.

In 1900, Planck proposed an equation for the explanation of his radiation problem, that has since found many applications including the spectrum. In quantum mechanics, radiation is absorbed and emitted in energy bundles Planck called quanta. Planck received a Nobel Prize in Physics in 1918.

In Einstein's two of four 1905 published papers made a change in the understanding of particles and waves. In his special theory of relativity, Einstein held the idea that matter is a form of energy. In his paper on the photoelectrical effect, Einstein explained the concept that electromagnetic radiation can behave as particles (photons). He received a Nobel Prize in Physics in 1921.

In 1909, Einstein was the first one to clearly present duality in physics as the concept of light, and that it could be a wave or a particle, and he used the particle point to explain it.

Geiger, (1911), at the suggestion of Rutherford, by using alpha (Helium nuclei) radiation waves, discovered the atomic nucleus of gold and of other substances.

In 1927, Heisenberg's work on wave and particle duality of matter and radiant energy was directed toward atomic and microscopic dimensions. If the position and velocity of an electron wave or particle needs to be known using quantum mechanics and Heisenberg's uncertainty principle, only an estimated position and velocity of the electron is obtained. The diffraction pattern of the electron is not specific in showing position and momentum, but shows evidence of the wave pattern. Heisenberg received a Nobel Prize in 1932 for his work in quantum mechanics.

In 1923, Compton explained the scattering of x-rays by electrons. Compton discovered in investigating the scattering of the x-rays by light with elements such as carbon there was an increase in wavelength. According to classical physics there should be no change. Compton realized the x-rays exhibited particle-like behaviors, collided with an electron, lost some of their energy in the process, and this would lower the frequency with a change of wavelengths produced in the secondary x-ray. This was proof of the dual nature of electromagnetic radiation, which means that it could behave as a wave and as a particle. Compton's precise predictions were fully confirmed by measurements made by Wilson's cloud chamber tracts. Compton and Wilson shared the 1927 Nobel Prize in Physics.

In 1924, de Broglie, influenced by Einstein's work, put forward the idea that particles behave as waves and waves behave as particles, and waves are within the atom. This was known as the wave-particle duality of particles and electromagnetic radiation. Depending on the type of experiment, either a wave or particle is used. Wavelength and frequency determine a particle's mass or momentum. De Broglie realized that duality should not be limited to radiation, and to include all matter. Davisson projected electrons at metal targets in a vacuum using a crystal that tested de Broglie's results and the experiments were in complete agreement. De Broglie received the Nobel Prize for Physics in 1929 for the wave nature of the electron.

Schrodinger, in 1925, succeeded in establishing his famous wave equation that when applied to the hydrogen atom obtained the same results as Bohr and de Broglie. It was for this work Schrodinger shared the 1933 Nobel Prize in Physics with Dirac. The next year, Schrodinger used waves with particles in equations similar to his wave equations to solve problems of electromagnetic radiation.

In 1927, Thompson performed experiments that revealed a diffraction pattern which provided evidence of the wave-particle duality of the electron. Thompson and Davisson shared the Nobel Prize in Physics in 1937 for their separate experimental discoveries of the diffraction of the electrons by crystals.

Fermi realized that Chadwick's neutron discovery in 1932 would be an excellent tool for creating new isotopes. Fermi and Segre bombarded uranium with slow neutrons producing new radioactive isotopes. Fermi received the 1938 Nobel Prize in Physics, and in his Nobel address actually referred to his production of elements 93 and 94 which he named ausonium (Neptunium) and hesperium (Plutonium).

Chapter 11

PARTICLES AND ANTIPARTICLES

When particles and antiparticles meet, they annihilate one another. Particles and antiparticles are always created or destroyed in equal numbers so the total electric charge in the universe remains constant. This balance is called symmetry.

The time interval that a particle and antiparticle exist is brief as they annihilate each other and disappear. The process can happen anywhere and at any time. The more massive the particle and the antiparticle, the shorter the time they exist. They are constantly being created and destroyed in the whole universe. The pairs exist for such short intervals that it is impossible to observe them, and for this reason they are called virtual pairs or virtual particles

When antimatter collides with ordinary matter it creates an explosion depending on the mass amount of the electrons and of the anti-electrons being annihilated; or changed from electrons to anti-electrons by changing charges and direction of travel.

Pair Annihilation: When a particle and an antiparticle meet, they annihilate each other and energy results. Matter is directly converted into energy. When an electron and its anti-electron (positron) annihilate each other, the result is gamma ray (photon) production.

Pair Production: The inverse of annihilation can occur; high energy can be converted directly to matter. If a gamma ray with a large amount of positive energy passes close to a nucleus, an anti-electron (positron) and electron can be produced (both are necessary as per the law of conservation of charges). The gamma ray disappears that produces the inverse action with the excess energy going into the positron and electron as kinetic energy. A massive particle such as an atomic nucleus must participate in the interaction so energy and momentum are conserved simultaneously. Then when the positron collides with another electron, they are annihilated, and the result is production of two or more photons or gamma rays depending on the amount of kinetic energy from the previous action.

Dirac, when studying particles in 1928, predicted the existence of antimatter when he mathematically applied Einstein's theory of relativity to electrons. Dirac's mathematical equations showed that an electron exists in two energy states, one state having positive energies and the other state having negative energies called an antiparticle, or as Dirac called it a positron.

In 1931, Dirac published his quantum theory of the electron stating for every particle there is also an antiparticle. The antiparticle has the same mass as the particle, but the charge is opposite, and it appears only in conjunction with a negatively charged electron; and a collision between them results in their annihilation. He reasoned that every particle had to have an antiparticle of opposite charge. Dirac added a new dimension to antimatter with the electron's antiparticle. Dirac's theory was confirmed the next year by Anderson. Dirac shared a Nobel Prize in Physics in 1933 with Schrodinger.

In 1932, Anderson with his cloud chamber discovered the positron. Anderson's cloud chamber photograph showed the paths of an electron and positron pair formed by the disintegration of a gamma ray photon. His discovery supported Dirac's theory that particles and their antiparticles exist. This experiment gave physical proof of Dirac's mathematical theory published a year earlier. It was figured if positrons were confirmed experimentally, then other antiparticles and antimatter existed. Anderson shared a Nobel Prize in Physics in 1936. Lamb and Rutherford noticed a tiny shift in the spectrum of light when they meet, even though they cannot be directly observed.

In 1948, Feynman, when working with Dirac's equation of electrons, reversed the direction in time: (1) an electron going backward was the same as anti-electron going forward, and (2) advanced waves and retarded waves might cancel without anti-matter and collapse. Feynman realized when an electron collides with an anti-electron they annihilate one another and create a gamma ray, but if reversed, the charge of an anti-electron becomes an electron going backward in time. In the electron and anti-electron annihilation process, the electron reversing direction becomes an anti-electron traveling backward in time.

In 1953, Glaser developed a bubble chamber to study reactions among high energy particles. When a charged particle passed through the superheated liquid under pressure, it formed ions along its path. Vapor bubbles formed on the ions, and with a reduction in pressure of the liquid, particles could be photographed. He received the 1960 Nobel Prize in Physics for his invention of the bubble chamber that has been improved and widely used.

In 1955, Segre and Chamberlain, with a powerful particle accelerator, created heavy antiparticles, and an antiproton of the nucleus of the hydrogen atom. Segre and Chamberlain were awarded the 1959 Nobel Prize in Physics for their work in demonstrating the existence of the antiproton.

Hawking studying pairs of particles, one of matter and one of antimatter, noted they meet and annihilate each other with no loss of energy.

Physicists working with sub-atomic particles were making particles and antiparticles using strong gamma rays, but discovered they must be made in pairs, one of each, that annihilate each other leaving only gamma rays. Pairs of virtual particles can be converted into real particles by high-energy gamma ray photons.

Now the production of matter and antimatter with particle accelerators is common.

Chapter 12

REACTORS, ACCELERATORS, COLLIDERS, AND CONFINEMENT SYSTEMS

In the 1900s, scientists were bombarding atoms with high energy particles to learn as much as possible about the nucleus. The nucleus has a positive charge that holds the electrons together and determines their energy status and wave patterns. The electron determines the chemical and physical properties of the atom. The atomic mass is in the nucleus. The strong nuclear force holds the nucleus together.

The first recorded artificial nuclear modification was by Rutherford in 1919 by alpha particles eliminating protons which were identified by magnetic deflection methods. Irene and Frederic Joliot-Curie (1934) redid the same experiments and found Rutherford missed the fact that radiation continued to be emitted from substances bombarded with alpha particles.

Conventional accelerators use fixed targets. Colliding beam accelerators called colliders use particles with equal masses and kinetic energies traveling in opposite directions in an accelerator ring to collide head-on to produce the formation of new particles.

Lawrence invented the cyclotron in 1920, and was awarded the 1939 Nobel Prize in Physics for the bombardment of the nucleus with the low energy accelerator. The cyclotron repeated a spiral course which produced several million electron-bolts of kinetic energy used for invasion and disrupting atomic nuclei. In 1931, Lawrence designed the cyclic accelerator to move charged particles in a spiral path under a vertical magnetic field of high frequency. Element lawrencium was named in Lawrence's honor.

Kerst (1930s) developed the betatron that accelerates electrons by using the principle of the transformer so electrons may be accelerated up to energies of many million electron volts in less than a thousandth of a second producing penetrating x-rays. The hollow doughnut-shaped tube of glass provides the path for the accelerated electrons. The betatron is used for the production of very penetrating x-rays and some nuclear changes. In 1955, the betatron particle accelerator at the University of California, Berkeley, produced its first antiproton.

At first fluorescent detectors were used as quantitative instruments such as the scintillation counter where the nuclei were bombarded by alpha particles from natural radioactive elements. Artificially accelerated particles are preferred as they offer some control over their energies and their numbers, such as the van de Graaff generator which in 1931 was developed as a particle accelerator. With the help of Trump, van de Graaff adapted the generator to produce high-energy x-rays for treatment of cancer in 1937.

In 1934, Einstein's equation showed that a single atom would produce only a small amount of energy, and therefore a large number of atoms would be needed to produce a large amount of energy to trigger others to release their energy. This is known as a chain reaction.

Hahn and Strassmann (1939) found by chemical analysis that barium and krypton appeared among the by-products of the bombardment of uranium with neutrons, and these two nuclei would result from the splitting of a nucleus of uranium. This kind of division was called nuclear fission, and could release unprecedented energy by neutrons producing a self-sustaining chain reaction in a mass of uranium.

Fermi produced and investigated the properties of a large number of newly created radioactive isotopes. Fermi directed his projection of slow neutrons into a nucleus producing a heavier nucleus that had an impact on the field of nuclear energy.

Fermi, in 1942, under U.S. government sponsorship, built a test structure to slow down the fast fission neutrons. Fermi used the racquet courts under the west stands of the University of Chicago's Stagg Field. Carbon bricks were built into a globular pole with six tons of uranium metal of high purity. Fermi and his colleagues stockpiled the first atomic pile of 40,000 graphite bocks in which some 22,000 holes were drilled to permit the insertion of several tons of uranium. Cadmium rods were inserted to absorb neutrons and control the reaction. The structure was large so the fission neutrons would complete their movements within it and not escape. The rods were removed at 3:45 pm, December 2, 1942. Fermi's stock pile had a chain reaction for twenty-eight minutes, the first self-sustaining chain reaction, and this initiated the controlled release of nuclear energy. Fermi was present when the first test bomb was exploded in the desert of New Mexico. Element Fermium was named in his honor.

Fermilab National Accelerator Laboratory, Batavia, Illinois, was named for Fermi. Breaking ground for construction was in 1968. In the Fermilab, particles are accelerated to four hundred to five hundred billion electron volts, and elementary particles can be accelerated to 99.99 percent of the speed of light. The Fermilab in 1996 produced one hundred atoms of anti-hydrogen. Later, a particle injector addition was built onto the Fermilab.

CERN is the acronym for the European Center for Nuclear Research which is located outside Geneva, also known as the Large Hadron Collider (LHC). Particles traveling at 99.94 per cent of the speed of light circulate in an orbit 40 feet in diameter, and are correct to within one part in 500. In 1995, CERN made history when it announced it had created nine anti-hydrogen atoms. Rubbia and van der Meer, working in different sections at CERN, received the 1984 Nobel Prize in Physics for their work on subatomic particles.

Another particle accelerator built in 2005 is the International Linear Collider (ILC). Instead of bending the path of subatomic particles into a circle like the Large Hadron Collider, the ILC shoots them down a straight path until they attain huge energies, then a beam of electrons will collide with anti-electrons into a beam of energy.

Experiments done at the Stanford Linear Accelerator Center, the Rutherford Appleton Laboratory in England, and the *Ecole Polytechniqe* in Paris show that enormous accelerations are possible within small distances using laser beams and plasma to inject energy. It has been demonstrated that double the energy can be obtained in just one meter, and then more by using a wave to give it an extra momentum.

The laser Shiva is the first attempt to create laser fusion. It is a twenty-beam laser system built at the Lawrence Livermore National Laboratory. In 1978, the Nova laser replaced the Shiva laser system with ten times the energy. Both failed to achieve the proper ignition with pellets.

There are two ways scientists are attempting to harness fusion on earth: (1). The Inertial Confinement for Fusion, and (2). The Magnetic Confinement for Fusion.

(1). The Inertial Confinement for Fusion uses a neodymium glass solid-state laser to duplicate the temperatures found in the core of a star, sufficient to fuse hydrogen nuclei into helium. It has a battery of 192 laser beams with an output of 700 trillion watts of power which can be concentrated in a single burst of energy. The National Ignition Facility (NIF) is located at the Lawrence Livermore National Laboratory.

(2). Magnetic Confinement for Fusion uses a process in which a hot plasma of hydrogen gas is contained within a magnetic field designed to heat hydrogen gas to 100 million degrees centigrade. It is designed to generate 500 megawatts of power for 500 seconds. The International Thermonuclear Experimental Reactor is being built in southern France by a group of nations.

Chapter 13

SINGULARITY

The universe is composed of billions of galaxies throughout space and each contains billions of stars. Galaxies are moving apart, toward and away from the earth as the universe expands. Singularities exist in all fields known or unknown within anything visible or invisible in the universe. Singularities are found in the collapsing of stars, and can be in space and time, and everywhere in our universe.

A singularity is a point in space and time at which the space-time curvature becomes infinite. Einstein joined together space and time as expressed in his 1905 special theory of relativity. Einstein's 1916 general theory of relativity illustrates that space-time can warp or bend. He mathematically calculated singularity in his general theory of relativity.

Schwarzschild and Kerr both have a singularity at the center in their black holes; and this region is cut off from the outside. Schwarzschild discovered singularity was a finite radius. Schwarzschild calculated the singularity radius of the sun which is now referred to as the Schwarzschild radius or gravitational radius.

Penrose proposed in his cosmic censorship hypothesis that a singularity produced by a gravitational collapsing black hole or star is inside and is unseen from the event horizon; this is the weak cosmic censorship hypothesis. The strong cosmic censorship hypothesis states a singularity would always be either entirely in the future or entirely in the past, like in the beginning of the universe, the big bang theory.

Penrose and Hawking worked with singularity theorems and showed that a singularity was a point of infinite density and infinite curvature of space-time, and probably a singularity was the beginning of time. They also showed the singularity theorems indicate the gravitational field is strong.

In 1965, Hawking read Penrose's theorem that a cosmic body undergoing gravitational collapse must eventually form a singularity. Hawking, in a moment of inspiration, realized the direction of time in Penrose's theorem could be reversed and the collapse would become an expansion. Penrose's theorem required the universe to be infinite in space. During the next four years, Hawking developed new mathematical techniques and other technical conditions. The result was a publication in 1970 by Penrose and Hawking that proved there was a big bang singularity.

The big bang theory from a single singularity is hard to argue against with Einstein's theory of general relativity, Penrose and Hawking's subsequent theoretical support, the observational work of Penzias and Wilson, and Smoot analyzing the COBE generated map of the early universe with tiny temperature changes. With all the collected information, they proved to their satisfaction our galaxy was created from a singularity verifying the big bang theory.

Chapter 14

GRAVITATIONAL AND STELLAR COLLAPSING STARS: SCHWARZSCHILD BLACK HOLES AND KERR BLACK HOLES

Einstein in his general theory of relativity mathematically presented collapsing stars. The stars, whether they are contracting, collapsing, or exploding are dealing with energy.

Black holes range from very tiny microscopic size and primordial size that are not larger than an atom to stellar black holes that are formed when a giant star collapses. The stellar collapse to form black holes must have a solar mass over 3.2.

Stars with less than 1.4 solar mass (mass of the sun) will collapse over millions of years into white dwarfs of low mass that cool and eventually become brown dwarfs. They are unable to generate energy, and pack themselves into balls about the size of the earth. Brown dwarfs are cold iron stars that do not emit light.

Stars over 1.4 solar mass but less than 3.2 solar mass are usually created when a star explodes such as a supernova, have a solid surface, or are called neutron stars that when rotating emit radio pulses, show density, magnetism, and extreme temperature.

Stars must be over 3.2 solar mass in order to become stellar collapsing stars when their fuel runs out, and become what is now called black holes. Stars larger than 3.2 solar mass often explode and throw off mass to avoid collapse.

Stellar stars have a force of gravity pulling inward which is held in check by pressure from the nuclear furnace in the center of the star which supplies the fuel of hydrogen changing into helium for the heat and light of the star.

When a star's fuel is gone, it will be overcome by its gravitational field, and become a stellar gravitational collapsing star eventually to collapse to zero size and infinite density as it becomes what is called a black hole.

All collapsing stars lose their characteristics to the black hole including mass, electrical charge and motion. The star's matter contracts to infinite density and infinitesimal volume in the black hole. The singularity and matter become heavy and gravity concentrates it in the bottom of the black hole where it is drawn through the black wormhole then through the white wormhole and into the white hole, where the concentration of matter can form a new luminous star which can leave into the universes' space-time or can leave as a singularity. The original gravitational collapsing star eventually collapses completely and disintegrates into cosmic ash.

Collapsing non-spinning stars above 3.2 solar mass become Schwarzschild black holes, and collapsing spinning stars above 3.2 solar mass become Kerr black holes. The positive energy of the collapsing star is balanced by the flow of negative energy particles into the black hole.

Einstein in his general theory of relativity published an understanding of energy-mass, and that gravity was a curving or warping of space-time. He also figured a mathematical description of a collapsing star that astronomers had observed.

Schwarzschild, an astronomer and theorist, was serving as an artillery officer in World War I. He obtained a copy of Einstein's 1916 general theory of relativity, and wrote three papers on the theory: two papers from the Russian Front, and one from a Berlin hospital where he was suffering with a rare fatal skin disease.

Schwarzschild calculated two mathematical proofs of Einstein's approximate solutions to his 1916 general theory of relativity. Einstein used 16 complex field equations; instead Schwarzschild used mass as an infinitesimal point for his finalizing Einstein's suggested equations. Schwarzschild saw space curvature of space-time and the red-shift as infinite; and the light waves as infinitely long to be completely cut off from the exterior region of a star.

Schwarzschild sent his first paper to Einstein from the Russian Front in December 1915. Einstein wrote back on January

9, 1916 thanking him for the exact solution so quickly. Schwarzschild sent a second paper to Einstein with the solution of the interior region of a collapsing star. Einstein presented both of Schwarzschild's papers just as he wrote them to the Prussian Academy for publication.

Schwarzschild's third paper calculated the singularity at the center of a black hole, and also at the finite radius, and found the region inside the singularity was cut off from the outside world. As a check on his computations, he calculated the singularity's radius of the sun. Schwarzschild sent his third paper to Einstein who submitted the work to the Prussian Academy for publication just as Schwarzschild presented it; and it became known as the gravitational radius or Schwarzschild radius.

Four months later in May 1916, Schwarzschild died at age forty-one. Einstein gave the obituary which was printed in the Prussian Journal together with Schwarzschild's last three published scientific papers that Einstein sent in for him.

Droste, working for Lorentz in 1917, was studying black holes in Einstein's general theory of relativity, and came up with the same solutions as Schwarzschild. In the same year, Flamm looked at the curved space around the singularity and discovered that it looked like a funnel; and when Weyl looked at it, he thought there was a funnel on each end.

Oppenheimer wrote the first comprehensive description of the collapse of dying stars in 1929. Oppenheimer wrote on a collapsing star noting once the radiation escaped the enormous increase in pressure in gravity accelerated the collapse. As the star collapsed, its light and energy would be reduced, gravity would continue, wavelengths would be shifted beyond the red end of the spectrum, and the star would close off in a gravitational collapse. When a star exhausts its thermonuclear fuel and gravity forces the star to collapse, it reaches the Schwarzschild radius. They also calculated that a collapsing small star about the mass of the earth has the Schwarzschild radius. Oppenheimer's results proved what Einstein's equations had predicted in a star's collapse as a place in the universe that swallowed all the matter and light.

Wheeler assigned two students to re-do Oppenheimer's 1929 calculations because large calculators were available. At the 1963 Texas Conference on Relativity they presented their paper which was made into a book. The results were basically the same as Oppenheimer's calculations. Wheeler called a star's collapse a black hole.

In 1935, Einstein and Rosen decided to study the geometry of the space around the gravitation radius. They also found a funnel-shaped tunnel that was predicted earlier by Droste, and an open image on the other end predicted by Weyl. These tunnels soon became known as Einstein-Rosen bridges and later called wormholes in space. The problem that Einstein envisioned was with the singularity, light, and particles concentrated in the bottom of the black hole because energy-mass can not disappear, so there should be an escape route into another universe or star formation. Einstein's concept of the other end of the worm hole maintained there existed an opening to another universe. That meant matter could go through the black hole, two wormholes, and end in the white hole with an opening into the universe. Physicists now call this end a white hole or time-reversed black hole.

Penrose (1965), working on the fundamentals of black holes as a prediction of Einstein's mathematics, proved in the gravitational collapse of a large star that gravity would collapse the matter inward through the event horizon to a dense point called singularity which is of infinite density and space-time curvature inside the back hole; and nothing, not even light, can escape.

In 1969, Penrose described a mechanism for the extraction of energy from a Kerr black hole which rotates the same direction as the spin. Penrose demonstrated a body on the edge of the ergosphere above the event horizon splitting with one half falling into the event horizon and the other half escaping from the ergosphere with rotational energy being transferred to it with increased mass-energy. The energy would come from the spin of the black hole, and with the loss of energy it would spin slower. This meant energy could be extracted from the black hole.

Newman found a black hole that was spinning and it had a charge. It is referred to as a Kerr-Newman black hole.

Sciama was supervising Hawking's thesis in mathematics when he heard Penrose lecturing on Einstein's theorems. Sciama became instrumental in Penrose and Hawking working together.

Hawking and Penrose realized, according to the general theory of relativity, there must be a singularity of infinite density and space-time curvature within a black hole. The event horizon at the mouth of the black hole is sufficient to allow anything that goes into the black hole to begin concentrating and could exit into another region of the universe via a wormhole.

One of Hawking's first discoveries was primordial black holes, some microscopic in size, which he called mini black holes. Hawking's theory was that black holes are not necessarily black, and effectively emit energy. The temperature depends on the black hole's mass; the higher the mass the lower the temperature, and the lower the mass the higher the temperature. According to the Hawking radiation theory, when the black hole looses its mass the temperature increases, the surface area shrinks and this increases the surface temperature until it explodes into a burst of energy. Hawking confirmed radiation emitted by the black hole satisfied the quantum formula for the emission of radiation derived by Plank in 1900.

Hawking, Carter and Bardeen (1972) discovered there was a connection between black hole physics and thermodynamics, and this made it easier to prove black holes have a temperature. Black holes emit radiation irrespective of its rotation. Hawking predicted black holes could emit particles independent of its spin, and obey the laws of physics concerning energy and the second law of thermodynamics. Hawking showed particles of energy came from the black hole as it was radiating, and therefore it was giving off energy. Hawking's radiation theory solved the problem of temperature and thermodynamics.

Hawking proved Bekenstein's ideas on black holes was correct, and that black hole entropy was at the surface of the event horizon. Hawking's theorem was that the surface area of a black hole never decreases, and if two black holes merge the overall area would be greater than the combined areas of the two black holes, which is actually a concept in thermodynamics called entropy, and that the entropy of an isolated system always increases.

Hawking determined gravity around the black hole could generate matter and antimatter (an electron and its antimatter called a positron) when they meet they vanish in a flash of energy. But near a black hole one particle could vanish into the black hole leaving the other particle free. If the particle that falls into the black hole is a positron, it can be viewed as an electron tunneling out of the black hole backwards in time as it reverses its time direction and converts into an electron free to leave. If an electron has fallen into the black hole, it can be interpreted as a positron escaping by motion backward in time until just outside the black hole as its interaction with gravity of the black hole reverses its time direction and then it is free. Hawking figured black holes can have both positrons and electrons tunneling out of a black hole.

According to Feynman if a positron falls into the black hole, it can be viewed as an escaping electron tunneling out of a black hole backward in time. The interaction with the black hole's gravity reverses its time direction and converts it to an electron that can go free into the universe. On the other hand, if it appears an electron has fallen into the black hole, it can be interpreted as a positron escaping by motion backward in time until its interaction with the gravity just outside the black hole reverses its time direction and it is free to go into the universe. This is by the quantum theory that particles can tunnel out of a black hole governed by relativity. The region through which a particle must tunnel is thinner for a mini black hole, and radiates away its energy faster than large black holes

Hawking (1973) agreed with Zeldovich's findings that black holes, spinning or non-spinning, create radiation yielding temperature depending on the mass of the black hole. Small black holes radiate away their energy faster than big ones depending on their mass, which makes them radiate more intensely.

Press and Teukolsky (1973) noted when stars collapse they contract to infinite dimensions and infinite density as a singularity point in a Schwarzchild black hole, and to a singularity ring in a Kerr black hole.

THE SCHWARZSCHILD BLACK HOLE

The Schwarzschild black hole is formed by a collapsing, non-spinning, gravitational star over 3.2 solar mass that is running out of fuel turning into a non-spinning, non explosive, spherical black hole with its size depending on the original star's mass. The collapsing star is drawn through the static limit area into the opening of the black hole called an event horizon that is a one way into the black hole that contains a mass point called a singularity. The light surrounding the event horizon is bent and curved with all light beams being pulled by gravity together with the collapsing star into the black hole to the singularity. Gravity pulls the concentration of the collapsed star and singularity to the bottom of the black hole through the black wormhole and white wormhole into the white hole where it can become a new luminous star out into the universe. In the Schwarzschild black hole, the singularity is a point of infinite density and space-time curvature within the black hole.

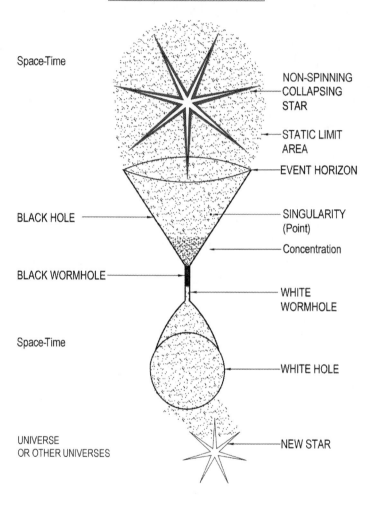

SCHWARZSCHILD BLACK HOLE

Space-Time

NON-SPINNING
COLLAPSING
STAR

STATIC LIMIT
AREA

EVENT HORIZON

BLACK HOLE

SINGULARITY
(Point)

Concentration

BLACK WORMHOLE

WHITE
WORMHOLE

Space-Time

WHITE HOLE

UNIVERSE
OR OTHER UNIVERSES

NEW STAR

THE KERR BLACK HOLE

The Kerr black hole is formed from a collapsing spinning gravitational star with a spin at a rate dependent on its size and shape, and gives off energy from rotation. As the spinning stellar star of 3.2 solar mass starts running out of fuel it collapses as a Kerr black hole, first meeting the static limit area where particles and light cannot remain at rest. The collapsing mass and light are then pulled around by the ergoshperes' spin frame dragging, and at this point they may be able to break free. The mass and light go through the two ergoshperes, then through the two event horizons to the black hole. If the rotation is slow, the spinning of the two ergoshperes are separate and spherical as is the same with the two event horizons; but with increased rotation the spinning of both of the ergospheres will merge together, and both of the event horizons will merge together, and the spins will change from spherical to elliptic shape. Energy can be extracted from light and particles breaking up in the ergospheres. If too much energy from the ergospheres is taken, the spinning will slow. The event horizons by their strong gravity can drag particles and light in the direction of its spin into the black hole where nothing can escape. The singularity inside the Kerr black hole is ring shaped. Gravity pulls the concentration of the singularity and mass drawing it through the black wormhole and white wormhole into the white hole where it forms a new luminous star that escapes into the universe.

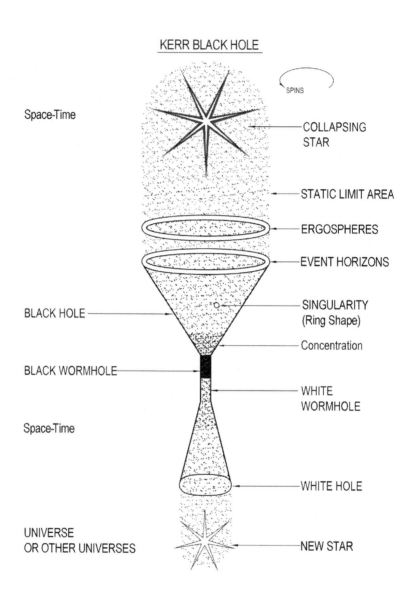

KERR BLACK HOLE

SPINS

Space-Time

COLLAPSING
STAR

STATIC LIMIT AREA

ERGOSPHERES

EVENT HORIZONS

BLACK HOLE

SINGULARITY
(Ring Shape)

Concentration

BLACK WORMHOLE

WHITE
WORMHOLE

Space-Time

WHITE HOLE

UNIVERSE
OR OTHER UNIVERSES

NEW STAR

Chapter 15

SPACE-TIME TRAVEL

Scientists studying Einstein's equations have found space-time solutions in the special theory of relativity for space-time travel.

Einstein proved that time could be at a different rate for different observers if the two observers were in relative motion or if one of them was in a much stronger gravitation field than the other.

In 1905, Rutherford and Soddy came to the conclusion that some chemical elements were being changed into other chemical elements; and they published their findings of special transformations.

Some work was done in 1937 by van Stockum showing a closed time loop that could act as a time machine.

In 1945, Feynman using electromagnetism and equations by Maxwell revealed that light has two solutions: first, a retarded wave that is the usual motion of light from one point to another point, and second, an advanced wave as the light goes backward in time.

A change of one element into another element is called transmutation; and it goes on spontaneously in all the natural radioactive elements. It can be neither accelerated nor prevented.

Godel, in 1949, worked on the construction of alternative universes that are models based on the general theory of relativity, and produced a rotating universe model. Godel discovered that a rotating universe could contain loops of closed time and this could be a possible space-time travel.

In 1957, Everett published an interpretation of quantum mechanics that it was possible for the universe to break off into parallel universes.

Bennett wrote an article on how teleportation was possible at the atomic level using the Einstein, Podolsky, and Rosen (EPR) experiment.

In 1997, Zeilinger showed that the quantum state of a particle could be transported. In teleportation, the particle is not transported but the information about the particle is scanned, transmitted to another point, and transferred to another particle that ends up an identical single particle. Teleportation is a big step. Some scientists think the Bose-Einstein condensate may also be used in a new type of teleportation.

Spatial-cloaking is when light is bent around an object in a way to make it disappear from view. Spatial-cloaking is possible because manipulations are possible with man-made substances called optical meta-materials made through nanotechnology. Temporal-cloaking is dealing with time and light; and the light problem has to be solved first before the temporal-cloaking dealing with time can be possible. It is said Friedmann produced fifty picoseconds of darkness experimenting with optic cable.

Hawking suggested if the universe was bendable and flexible, the universe could bend and fold back on itself; and if close enough, it could be linked by wormholes through space-time so we could move from one place in the universe through a wormhole to another place in the universe.

Krauss mentioned time travel has paradoxes and there must be a basic distinction between cause and effect and the future and the past.

Hawking put forth his chronology protection hypothesis that the laws of physics conspire to prevent time travel by macroscopic objects; and if time-space travel is impossible, it is important to understand why.

Space-time travel is being explored in many ways and is accepted as possible. Suggestions and investigations are interesting, intriguing, and challenging.

Kaku simply said that there will always be new horizons.

Chapter 16

THE QUANTUM THEORIES AND THE HEISENBERG UNCERTANTY PRINCIPLE

In 1900, Planck was searching for a solution on emission of radiation at all wavelengths from a heated object. Planck developed a new radiation formula called Planck's formula, and the emissions from radiation he named quanta. He needed a constant so introduced what he called elementary quantum of action. Planck published his work which became the quantum hypothesis. Soon physicists were using it and adding to it including Einstein, Bohr, and Compton. In 1918, Planck received the Nobel Prize in Physics for his work of the quantum theory and for the Planck constant.

Planck developed the quantum theory further, and Einstein improved it publishing a paper in 1907 on Planck's theory of radiation of solids. In 1909, Einstein showed by duality that light could be either a wave or particle in quantum mechanics.

In 1913, Einstein published two papers on the quantum theory and one on Planck's law of radiation. Bohr assumed electrons moved between energy levels, but did not pursue it so Einstein followed up on it showing two types of transitions were possible.

In 1913, Bohr, on the basis of the quantum data by Planck and data of spectral analyses, figured that electrons orbit the nuclei at specific distances within the atom. This is the classical Bohr atom. Bohr's model of hydrogen's electron orbiting the nucleus with no neutron supported the quantum mechanistic theory. It was soon used in microscopic work. Sommerfield, in

1916, modified Bohr's atomic model by proposing that electrons move in elliptical orbits. He also interpreted hydrogen's fine spectral lines by quantum numbers.

Einstein in 1914 wrote *Contributions to the Quantum Theory* which verified the quantum hypothesis.

In 1921, Bose became interested in Planck's radiation law that showed the radiation curve for a heated object could be explained by emission and absorption of heat that took place in quanta (photons). Prior to this it was thought to be a continuous process. Bose used both classical physics and quantum concepts. Einstein would have preferred he used only quantum concepts, therefore, Bose re-did his work using only quantum mechanics, and the results agreed with Planck's formula.

In classical physics the forces are transmitted by fields, and everything can be predicted, measured and weighted. Generally, in quantum theories, the forces are force fields that move between particles transmitting the force; and there are many possibilities with no specific measurements and weights.

In 1924, de Broglie presented his hypothesis of the dual nature of matter that all particles exhibit both wave and particle properties. He mathematically proved the dual nature of protons. De Broglie's idea that particles have a wave nature was soon used in quantum subatomic research. De Broglie worked on the quantum theory to update it with the concept that particles of energy are guided through space by a real wave, and exchange energy with a sub-quantum medium. In 1927, Davisson measured the wavelength of electrons and this provided the first experimental conformation of the matter waves proposed by de Broglie. De Broglie received the 1929 Nobel Prize in Physics for his discovery of the wave nature of the electron.

In 1925, Heisenberg formulated an addition to the quantum theory he called matrix mechanics. It was for this work Heisenberg received the 1932 Nobel Prize in Physics that was later shown to be equivalent to Schrodinger's wave mechanics.

In 1926, Schrodinger proposed a wave equation that described how matter waves change in space and time; a key tool in the theory of quantum mechanics. Physicists preferred to use Schrodinger's wave equation over Heisenberg's matrix mechanics. Schrodinger's wave equation is used with the wave movements of electrons and atoms, and is defined at every point in space and time. It was for this work he was awarded the 1933 Nobel Prize in Physics that was shared with Dirac.

As the wave particle duality of the electron and other ideas progressed, Heisenberg realized something was necessary to permit the correct prediction of atomic phenomena. In 1926, Heisenberg introduced his uncertainty principle that basically states it is impossible to know the exact position and momentum of any mass, object, field, or energy-mass wave during an instant of time especially during light's high velocity, and the exact energy measured over a given amount of time. With Heisenberg's uncertainty principle added to the quantum theory, physicists could now explain puzzling questions and some laws.

Most physicists and mathematicians using the uncertainty principle are concerned with microscopic subjects, waves, light, and electromagnetism. When using the Heisenberg uncertainty principle to calculate there are inaccuracies especially in the case of light. The uncertainty principle deals with these inaccuracies when the mathematics has more than one answer. The solution is called probabilities. With probabilities and extra dimensions, it is difficult to challenge a theory in quantum experimental research.

The Heisenberg uncertainty principal emphasizes duality, and that any particle field in motion can be expressed as a spinning wave as originally accepted in 1919 by Planck, Einstein, and de Broglie. The opposite charge attraction and the similar charge repulsion interaction are a basic ingredient of electromagnetic experiments.

In 1930, Dirac published his first edition of his classic work on the principles of the quantum theory in which he developed a general formalism. For this work he shared the 1933 Nobel Prize in Physics with Schrodinger.

Einstein supported and improved the quantum theory in the beginning, but he questioned it as it progressed and evolved allowing uncertainty. Later, Einstein stated that the quantum mechanistic equation represented one of the better achievements in the twentieth century, but Einstein thought there must be an improved solution. Most scientists accept and work with quantum mechanics and the Heisenberg uncertainty principle.

Feynman considered some of the problems in quantum electrodynamic (QED) interactions between electrons and photons. In classical physics theories, forces are transmitted by fields. In quantum field theories, the force fields are force carrying particles that move between particles of matter transmitting the force.

In 1949, Feynman introduced path integrals, also called sum over histories. Feynman's theory visualized wave particle duality. By using his sum over histories, the field had the possibility to move from point to point utilizing a number of routes, wave dynamics, and phases. Feynman's theory worked, and the results were the same as Schrodinger's wave functions.

Feynman then showed how to calculate these path integrals using what is called Feynman's diagrams. Feynman's graphical diagrams provided a way of illustrating sum over histories; and are an important tool with lines and vertices in each diagram as a mathematical expression. It was for this basic work in quantum electrodynamics he shared the Nobel Prize in Physics in 1965.

It was soon realized discoveries made years earlier by Wilson, and equations by Wheeler, could be helpful in visualizing the quantum results, and made clearer the understanding of quantum gravity.

The gravitational effects are important in the quantum theory of gravity. There is a need to combine the general theory of relativity with the quantum theory of gravity, and it may include Feynman sum over histories and Einstein's gravitational field of space-time.

In 1980, Sen attempted to quantize a theory of supergravity, and his breakthrough was suited for quantum calculations. The quantum gravity's important results were that Planck lengths were quantized with the minimum allowed volume, and all other volume numerical multiples of it.

The quantum theory has been a success in most scientific endeavors and technology in all of its probabilities except in gravity and large-scale structures of the universe. The quantum mechanistic theory equations are most useful applied to atomic and subatomic research.

The quantum hypothesis and quantum mechanics theory has developed and grown to include many branches that include research on many different ideas, information transmissions, quantum entanglement, and teleportation probable at the atomic level. The microscopic and macroscopic scientists have had good results.

Quantum mechanics works with antimatter, sub-atomic, and nuclear physics. Quantum chromo dynamics theory (QCD) studies include quark interactions. Quantum electrodynamics theory (QED) studies include interactions of electrical charges.

There seems to be no limit or boundaries to the opportunities and challenges of the quantum theories

Chapter 17

THE STRING THEORY

The string theory has had an interesting development beginning with the string theory to the superstring theory to the M-theory.

At first two theories, the string theory and the quantum loop gravity theory were searching for solutions to the same fundamental ideas. They were two ways of looking at the same problem with the string theory receiving the most support.

The foundation for the atomic string theory is vibrating ultra small energy strings that are one dimensional. Strings can join together to form a single string or can divide, open or join ends. In the string theory, the vibrating strings compose all masses, force charges, and energies within the atom. The shorter the vibrating string the greater the mass.

A particle occupies one point of space in time. A string occupies one line in space at a moment of time. The string theorists generally use the quantum mechanistic equation on a non-mechanistic point instead of Einstein's mechanistic point changed to a field equation. The reasoning is the quantum mechanistic equation can be used on a string that is not on a mechanistic point when the strings join other strings, and may become as long as an atom.

Veneziano published a paper on the dual resonance of interactions using point particles. In 1968, Veneziano and Suzki published a formula on the movement of vibrating or resonance strings in subatomic particles.

In 1970, Nambu proposed that elementary particles may not be particles at all, but could be vibrating, rotating, strings with energy proportional to their length.

In 1970, Nambu, Susskind and Nielson studying dual resonance found that strings could vibrate with different resonance like the strings of a guitar. They found that resonance of a string could describe one of the two elementary particles called bosons. They accounted for bosons, and Raymond soon accounted for the other elementary particle called fermions. Bosons are particles that transmit force, and fermions are matter particles, and together they are referred to as exchange particles.

Scherk and Schwarz in 1974 realized the string theory had the properties of graviton, and published a paper on the gravitational force and the string's tension.

Neveu and Schwarz improved the string theory by reducing the dimensions from twenty-six to ten; but the theory still had trouble with the speed of light. Schwarz then worked on ideas in Nambu's original proposal.

In 1976, Scherk's group discovered it may be possible to incorporate supergravity into the string theory. Supergravity is an extension of the general theory of relativity plus symmetry has been added. Superstrings are used for calculating high energy particles, and supergravity is used for calculating large particles as in space curvatures and matter that is Einstein's theory of curved space-time. Supergravity has low energy and easily combines the four forces of the universe into the string theory. Supergravity has eleven dimensions referred to as point particles. There are equal numbers of bosons and fermions therefore they cancel out in the supergravity theory.

Supersymmetry was formulated by Wess and Zumino, not for the string theory but for point particles. They were interested in two types of particles namely fermions and bosoms. By applying symmetry principles, they mathematically could change boson into fermions and fermions into bosons, and called it supersymmetry.

Supersymmetry helped combine the quantum theory and the general theory of relativity theory, and smoothed the curved space needed in general relativity. The addition of supersymmetry gave another tool for physicists working on a grand unified theory, or the union of the general theory of relativity and the quantum theory.

The addition of supersymmetry into the string theory was a major breakthrough; it made the combination of the string theory and supersymmetry to be known as the superstring theory.

Glashow, Salam and Weinberg showed electromagnetic and weak forces were connected. In 1974, Glashow showed that the electromagnetic, weak and strong forces had the same strength in the early universe; and when supersymmetry was added to their theory, the three forces became equal at short distances.

Schwarz and Green started to work together in 1979, and in 1981 published a string theory that contained supersymmetry, had no infinities, explained all four forces of the universe, and seemed to predict the elementary particles, but was not anomaly free. In 1982 to 1984, Schwarz and Green's interest continued in the string theory, and in 1984, they published their work as a version of the string theory that was anomaly-free.

A few months later other anomaly free theories were presented. The sizes of the strings were decreased when gravity was included in the theory. There were problems with the equations, and the solutions were approximate.

In 1984, Witten was working on his M-theory and took note of Schwarz and Green's work, and using a different approach showed the theory was indeed anomaly free.

Witten, at a conference in Los Angeles in 1995, presented his M-theory. Witten showed his five string theories of the superstring theory were five different ways of the same theory using dualities. Dualities showed the five superstring theories were physically equivalent to supergravity. The superstring theory was basically the same as supergravity. The five theories were different expressions of the same theory as Witten linked the five superstring theories by dualities which resulted in one M-theory.

In Witten's M-theory of five theories and eleven dimensions, Klein and Kaluza thought of curling up a single dimension to look like a cylinder. Witten, in 1984, took the superstring theory's dimensions and curled them up in Calabi-Yau shapes at each point in space. One of the eleven dimensions was actually a tube and became a two dimensional membrane, leaving ten dimensions. Witten now had six theories which he linked to one M-theory with the curling up of the ten dimensions in superstring theory by dualities. All four forces (gravitational, strong, weak and electromagnet) came together and were of equal value. The energy of the strings came from vibration motion and winding energy.

The M-string theory is a modification of the superstring theory and supergravity using dualities. Witten was awarded the 1990 Fields Metal for his work in pure mathematics and physics.

Hawking considered the dualities of the superstring theory good for calculations, and the M-theory good for calculations of high energy small particles; and the supergravity good for describing energy of large particles, basically Einstein's theory of curved space-time matter.

The string theory, in the opinion of some scientists, is a field theory. To prove this to their satisfaction, they claim all they need to do is use the word "field" in place of the word "string" in the string theory.

The string theory, superstring theory, and the M-string theory have been difficult to explain with experimental tests and mathematical computations. Some scientists accept the string theories and others do not, regardless it remains an accepted, possible structure of the atom. It has had variable support as the theory of everything, and frequent abandonments, but it endures with possibilities.

Chapter 18

$E=mc^2$ and $E=\pm mc^2$

The initial equation, $E=mc^2$, was published in the *Annals of Physics* as Einstein's fourth paper of 1905, *Does the Inertia of a Body Depend on its Energy Content?* It was only two pages long.

The profound formula only contains energy, mass, and light: E is for energy, m is for mass, and c is the speed of light squared. The amount of mass that is gained or lost is going to be balanced by the equivalent amount of energy that is gained or lost. Einstein's linking energy via the speed of light, and relating mass and energy, was a tremendous insight.

In 1916, Dirac noticed a mathematical $\pm$ was required in Einstein's equation, and corrected Einstein's equation of $E=mc^2$ to $E=\pm mc^2$. Dirac sent this correction as a paper to Einstein in 1916, and Einstein sent it for publication to the Prussian Academy, thereby Dirac's revision formally introduced $E=\pm mc^2$, and it became known as the Dirac-Einstein equation.

Einstein's equation of $E=mc^2$ and the Dirac-Einstein revision of $E=\pm mc^2$ are both considered universal standard scientific equations.

Initially the Dirac-Einstein's $E=\pm mc^2$ equation appeared to some as an outlandish skeptical idea, but harsh comments were abruptly changed when the positron was discovered in 1932. Dirac had predicted the positron as the electron's antiparticle one year earlier. The positron was discovered by Anderson with his cloud chamber in 1932 for which he received a Nobel Prize in 1936.

Einstein with his $E=\pm mc^2$ equation introduces the image of everything in the universe, and it can be used for everything experimental, mathematical and theoretical.

$E=mc^2$ is the most universally known and used equation in the world.

Chapter 19

EINSTEIN'S COSMOLOGICAL CONSTANT

Einstein believed Newton's idea of an infinite, static and unchanging universe. He thought local variations such as space-time was affected by mass, but the status of the universe remained the same.

Shortly before Einstein formulated his general theory of relativity in 1916, his equations showed the universe was moving, and an antigravity force had an expanding effect on space-time. Einstein used a cosmological constant to counteract the antigravity forces in his equations to show a static state of the universe in which he believed at the time.

Friedmann in 1922 pointed out the universe is not static, and proved it mathematically. Friedmann redid Einstein's cosmological equation adjustment without the constant with surprising results, and sent it to Einstein who forwarded it for publication making one correction which was not correct, and then sent a note of correction with his error to the publisher.

In 1931, Hubble published that all but the nearest galaxies were moving away, and the universe was expanding. Hubble agreed with the theory proposed by Lemaitre and with Friedmann's expanding universe reported in 1922. In 1927, Lemaitre used Einstein's general theory of relativity to describe an exploding universe.

At Lemaitre's lecture that Einstein attended with Hubble, Einstein realized the world was not static as he had believed, and orally withdrew his cosmological constant in 1927; and said it was his worst mistake. Einstein withdrew his cosmological constant, in writing in 1931, as unnecessary and compromising the simplicity of his field equations.

In 1932, Falco, Kochanek, and Munoz showed by using Einstein's cosmological constant the number of quasars that were lensed had increased. The cosmological constant helped them account for about sixty-two per cent of the energy density (dark energy) of the universe.

Einstein missed an opportunity by not re-studying and re-evaluating his abandoned cosmological constant as it is presently being used as a tool in many concepts. Astronomers are using Einstein's cosmological constant to explain the expansion of the universe. Physicists in quantum electrodynamics studying interactions of particles and radiation are also using Einstein's cosmological constant. It is being used wherever it is applicable.

Chapter 20

EINSTEIN'S GRAVIATATIONAL LENS AND EINSTEIN'S RINGS

An Einstein gravitational lens needs a background object (such as a star), a deflector (such as another star, dark matter, or a black hole), and a telescopic observer on earth. Quasars and distant galaxies are good background objects because of their distance from the earth which makes them likely to have objects between them and the viewer. If the deflector and the background object are exactly aligned with the viewer, the viewer will see a ring which will be an enlarged image of the background object with the deflector in the center. If two objects are closely aligned but slightly off, the viewer will see two images as crescents or points of light.

One of the best gravitational lens effects is the Einstein ring. It is a complete circle of light with the deflector at the center that requires a perfect alignment of the background object and the deflector so the rays from the background object bend around the deflector symmetrically.

In 1911, Einstein was at the forefront of the discovery. He worked out the details of gravitational lenses, and predicted that distant objects would be magnified if there was an exact alignment. He even predicted that several images would be seen if the alignment was slightly off. When a star is behind a massive object, its light rays will be bent as they pass the object, with the object acting as a lens. The gravitational lens technique has proven to be of value in detecting structures and items in the universe.

The chance of a gravitational lens occurring at any time is rare. Several such occurrences have been observed with the Hubble telescope. If a star passes in front of a quasar as it moves closer to perfect alignment, the quasar image will break up into two or more images, but as perfect alignment occurs, a ring will appear, and it will eclipse one image at a time.

Einstein rings can be used to assist in understanding mass distribution in galaxies. In some cases the gravitational lens is not of a single galaxy but a cluster of galaxies showing a large number of arcs. The arcs are helpful in that they are from galaxies we would not be able to see if not using a gravitation lens procedure. Gravitational lenses can also be used in the study of dark matter found in a cluster of galaxies.

Refsdal worked out the mathematics for several applications of gravitational lenses; and he showed it is a useful tools in astronomy including determining Hubble's cosmology constant.

King and several colleagues found an almost perfect circular ring plus a bright central galaxy using a radio source. Radio astronomers do not need a dark sky to use their radio telescopes.

Hubble's constant is one of the most important constants in cosmology. It shows information about the age and the size of the universe. The Hubble constant procedure involves many complicated mathematical steps to obtain the results, and if one step is missed the whole calculation needs to be redone.

Refsdal showed that Einstein's gravitational lens can be used in calculating age and size instead of using the Hubble constant. The Hubble constant is the ratio of two numbers, and the calculation is based on the slight difference in time that it takes for light signals from the two images to reach us. The gravitational lens calculation is a result of the slightly different paths the two light rays take and the gravitational field of the lens' object. The values obtained from the gravitational lens calculations are slightly lower but workable compared to the complicated long Hubble constant method.

Einstein's gravitational lens has become a major tool in astronomy. It has proven to be of considerable value in cosmology for detecting structures of quasars and galaxies, the mass distribution of galaxies, and in the search for dark matter;

and also in calculating age and size of objects in the universe instead of using the Hubble constant.

Chapter 21

SOLVAY COUNCIL AND THE GEDANKEN
EXPERIMENT

The Solvay Councils were a series of international
conferences for physicist held in Brussels, Belgium. The
conferences were started and financed by Ernest Solvay, a
Belgium industrial chemist, for the exchange of nuclear,
quantum, and current information. The first Solvay Council was
held in 1911 discussing light bent by acceleration, and the
amount of light falling upon the earth in one second.

Einstein and Bohr were among those that attended the
1927 Solvay Council. Attendees had conference sessions during
the day and discussions in the evenings. At an evening
discussion, Bohr was explaining what Einstein considered a
wrong direction taken in quantum mechanics. Einstein thought a
particle was not real until it was measured; and he had
reservations on other new aspects of the theory also.

In 1930, at the Sixth Solvay Council, there were many
challenges and discussions over the applicability of the quantum
mechanistic theory. Einstein presented a demonstration he
thought would make the Heisenberg uncertainty principle
inapplicable. Einstein, utilizing his Gedanken experiment,
predicted that the position and velocity of an electron could be
determined.

Einstein's experiment had electrons in a container with a
shutter which opened and closed instantaneously that permitted
one electron to leave the container capturing it in a connected
container, and thus the first container would weigh one electron
less.

Einstein figured knowing the equivalence of matter and energy would give him the total energy the first box contained without any uncertainty, and therefore it would prove the uncertainty principle was wrong. Weighing the one electron and calculating the weight of the box and its position could also be determined. Bohr was stunned and Einstein was confident.

But the next morning, Bohr stated according to the general theory of relativity that one could never determine the container's mass accurately as the container's movement would not permit it. Bohr said the box weighed less because of gravity, the uncertainty of the shutter time would be translated into measuring the position of the box, therefore the uncertainty in position of the box and the uncertainty in the weight of the box would reflect in its energy, and the experiment would agree with the uncertainty principle. Bohr won the debate and Einstein congratulated Bohr.

The uncertainty of it all gave Bohr the upper hand, and prestige for the quantum theory. Later, Einstein recommended that Schrodinger and Heisenberg share a Nobel Prize in Physics.

Chapter 22

THE QUANTUM MECHANICS CHALLENGE

Einstein did not agree with the new concepts and the direction that quantum mechanics was taking, so he took time to look at the fundamentals again. He wanted to prove the incompleteness of the quantum mechanics theory.

In 1935, Einstein, Podolsky and Rosen published their paper in *Physical Review* entitled *Can Quantum Mechanical Description of Physical Reality Be Considered Complete?* questioning the quantum theory's reality, completeness, and possible hidden variables, dealing with the position of a particle and its momentum. It was soon referred to as the EPR paper. Heisenberg, Pauli, and Bohr did not appreciate the article, Bohr published a response, and most scientists accepted the quantum theory. Einstein continued to work on the difficulties he realized in quantum mechanics, and published them in 1948 and 1949.

In 1949, Neumann published proof that hidden variables did not exist, and thought quantum mechanics was a viable theory.

In 1956, Bell showed Neumann's proof was invalid, and that the Einstein, Podolsky and Rosen paper was not necessarily wrong.

By this time the question was no longer a thought experiment but one of experimentation. In 1969, Bell realized a test was necessary to determine if the quantum theory was incomplete or not. The three main issues of the paper were completeness, reality and locality.

Shimony and Horne together and Clauser separately set up guidelines for the research challenge. Shimony and Horne lined up Holt and his colleagues to be on one team, and Clauser and Freedman agreed to be on another team. Both teams worked independently with different results. Holt and his colleagues came to the conclusion that Einstein was correct. Clauser and Freedman's conclusion was that their research supported quantum mechanics.

A more exact and precise experiment was needed. In 1974, Aspect designed three experiments, each based on a different principle, and each using pairs of entangled photons. Physicists and scientists were sincerely interested and concerned in the results. The results showed Einstein's locally and hidden variables were incorrect, and quantum mechanics was correct.

Then other scientists came up with their experimental results: Mandel used lasers, Gisin used optical cables, and Shih did his experiments, and all showed quantum mechanics was considered to be complete.

Chapter 23

MATHEMATICS OF THE NON-SYMMETRIC FIELD

Einstein's approach to mathematics was different. First Einstein would think about an experiment and then picture it in his mind with the events that would affect it or limit it, and then formulate a mathematical equation that completed the picture.

When Einstein started to write the general theory of relativity on gravitation, Planck warned Einstein not to include a section on gravitation. Planck told Einstein that no one would believe his concepts of gravitation and it would be a mistake. Einstein maintained that his general theory of relativity was mathematically concerned with gravitation.

In 1916, Einstein proposed his general theory of relativity including gravity and space-time curvature. Einstein used the equivalence of inertial and gravitational mass mathematically in the general theory of relativity; and also concepts of space-time and energy-mass. In his theory, Einstein explained space-time determined the shell orbit atomically of any energy-mass.

Some scientists had difficulty in understanding and applying Einstein's theory of gravity in his 1916 general theory of relativity. In 1954, Einstein worked to clarify his generalization of gravitation theory, and accomplished it in part in collaboration with his assistant, Kaufman. They succeeded in simplifying the derivatives as well as the form of the field equations so Einstein's relativistic theory of the non-symmetric field became clearer without changing its content.

The results were printed by Einstein as Appendix II in the fifth edition of his book, *The Meaning of Relativity Including the*

Relativistic Theory of the Non-Symmetric Field, (December 1954). Appendix II comprised ten mathematic equations with explanations added to the fifth edition so Einstein's generalization of gravitation theory became more understandable without changing the theory.

In his book, at the end of Appendix II, Einstein shared his observations, suggestions, and comments for physicists and mathematicians to consider or study.

Einstein and Kaufman's work was published in *The Annals of Mathematics* (June 29, 1954) entitled *Algebraic Properties of the Field in the Relativistic Theory of the Asymmetric Field*; and then published in *Annals of Mathematics* (July 1955), revised in more detail, as *A New Form of The General Relativistic Field Equations.*

The addition of Appendix II by Einstein to his fifth edition of his general theory of relativity and the two publications by Einstein and Kaufman were the last written and submitted before Einstein's death on April 18, 1955.

At the 50th Anniversary Conference on Relativity held at Bern, Switzerland, July 11-16, 1955 (after Einstein's death), Kaufman presented Einstein's work in which she participated entitled *The Mathematical Structure of the Non-Symmetric Field Theory.*

Chapter 24

ALBERT EINSTEIN'S CAREER AND LIFE

SUMMARY OF EINSTEIN'S SCIENTIFIC CAREER

Einstein's contributions to the scientific world are outstanding. Words alone cannot assess the scientific and mathematical contributions of Einstein.

During his lifetime, Eisenstein wrote close to three hundred books, papers, introductions, forwards, prefaces, and remembrances. His contributions remain the standard for achievements.

Einstein visualized everything in his mind conceptually, simply, vastly, and completely. Einstein believed to determine the future everything about the past and present should be known and used. Einstein's ability to think was his best tool.

In 1905, Einstein published four papers in the German journal *Annalen der Physik (Annals of Physics)*. These four papers remarkably changed physics. In the first of the four papers, Einstein presented a formula for displacement of particles in suspension. It was for the second of the four papers Einstein received the Nobel Price in Physics in 1921 declaring light consisted of particles. In the third of the four papers, Einstein introduced his special theory of relativity; and in the fourth paper presented $E=mc^2$.

Scientists may publish one paper or a book as a sole author in a year, but Einstein in 1905, who majored in physics was not an established scientist but a clerk in a patent office, published four papers in a noted physics journal in one year that were significant, especially his special theory of relativity and his

E=mc² equation of everything, and the second paper of the four later won a Nobel Prize. Einstein's four papers in 1905 influenced the direction of physics and science.

Among Einstein's many great accomplishments were these four papers in 1905 called his "Annus Mirabilis" or "Miracle Year."

Three of Einstein's scientific papers published in November of 1915 were combined and published as a book the next year as Einstein's 1916 general theory of relativity. Scientists had difficulty understanding some of Einstein's general theory of relativity, especially the section on gravitation. In 1954, Kaufmann worked with Einstein to clarify it without changing its content or meaning. The results were printed by Einstein as Appendix II in the fifth edition of his general theory of relativity,

Einstein's equation $E=mc^2$ was beyond reality. The most prominent and valuable contributions to physics and the world are Einstein's special theory of relativity, general theory of relativity, gravity waves, and his E=mc² equation. E=mc² is the only equation in the world that includes everything.

Einstein always had time to help other scientists publish their work submitting it in their name. When their work had quality but rejected for publication, Einstein, when asked, corrected it, added to it, and then submitted it for publication in their name; and if his contribution was substantial, submitted it with permission in both names.

Many scientists have utilized Einstein's ideas progressing science. The Bose-Einstein condensate has been utilized for laser beams. Ketterle produced atoms that acted like the superatoms that Einstein produced years earlier taking superfluidity all the way to absolute zero to make superatoms, and he called them a new form of matter. Schrodinger pursued a theory that Einstein had discarded and unified light and gravity.

There were many ideas Einstein did not use, pursue, or discarded that were successfully used by others; and often their work increased the knowledge of physics and they were awarded Nobel Prizes.

Einstein stated, concerning his united field theory, he was certain about the mathematical concepts of his theory but still uncertain about the physical aspects. Einstein's goal was to create a unified theory of everything, but it was left undone.

In addition to his many books, theories, papers, and ideas in his life time, he gave numerous lectures and tributes, and wrote multiple letters many of which have been collected and published as books

Others have stated that Einstein wished to think like God, but Einstein knew no one can think like another person, and to think like God can only be wishful thinking.

SUMMARY OF EINSTEIN'S LIFE

Albert Einstein was born on March 14, 1879, in Ulm, Germany, of Jewish parents, Hermann and Pauline Koch Einstein. They had an older daughter, Maja. When Einstein was five years old, his father gave him a compass, and Einstein marveled how it reacted. At the age of six years old, he started taking violin lessons, and taught himself to play the piano. He was an avid reader of books on mathematics, science, and technology. He taught himself calculus. Einstein failed his military induction test because of flat feet, excessive foot perspiration and varicose veins. He relinquished his German citizenship; and he applied and received Swiss citizenship a few years later. He could write elegant and beautiful prose. Einstein received his doctorate from the University of Zurich.

Einstein had difficulty relating to his teachers and professors, and had trouble obtaining recommendations from them for a job. A friend's father helped Einstein get a job at the Swiss Patent Office as a clerk.

While working in the patent office, Einstein studied, read and wrote scientific papers in the evenings. He published his first paper in 1904, and then his four publications in 1905. Few readers understood Einstein's concepts as applied to mechanistic points. Recognizing Einstein's 1904 published contributions to physics, Planck sent his assistant (von Laue who received a Nobel Prize in Physics for his work in 1914) to met Einstein working in the Swiss Patent Office in Bern in 1906. Once Einstein's work was recognized by Planck, Einstein's professional career developed as a theoretical physicist; and over his life time he held positions at universities in Bern, Zurich, Prague, Utrecht, and Berlin.

Einstein's father, on his deathbed, gave Einstein permission to marry Mileva Maric Maritsch, a fellow physics student. Einstein and Mileva had two sons, but their marriage ended after ten years with Mileva leaving Berlin returning to Zurich in 1915 with their two sons. Later, Einstein gave Mileva the Nobel Prize money he was awarded to care for her and their two sons. Einstein's relatives lived in Berlin, and after a short time he married his cousin, Elsa.

In 1917, Einstein suffered from gastrointestinal problems loosing 56 pounds. By December, Einstein developed an abdominal ulcer and was confined to bed for several months. In Zurich, Milvea and Eduard were ill and both hospitalized, so Einstein sent more than half of his salary to Milvea, Eduard and Hans. In 1918, Einstein was too weak to submit his own scientific papers, so his colleagues submitted his papers for him. Elsa was instrumental in nursing Einstein back to health.

While visiting King Albert's uncle, Caesar, Einstein met Queen Elizabeth of Belgium. The queen, a lady-in-waiting, and Einstein played a musical trio together. The Queen and Einstein had a warm friendship with Einstein writing to her until the end of his life. Einstein corresponded with many friends and scientists over the years and many of his letters have been collected and published.

With anti-Semitism growing, Einstein made two speaking tours in the USA and one in Japan. When Einstein went to England, he met the British Prime Minister at a dinner who wrote on his card asking for Einstein's address, and Einstein indicated he had no address.

The Third Reich verbally condemned Einstein and his writings, and put a price on his head. Jewish scientists were harassed, and the Nazis burned scientific books written by Jews, and scientists that were not Nazis. Scientists of Jewish decent were leaving Germany as their lives were in danger. When the Nazis, with Hitler as Chancellor, came into power, Einstein and Elsa were in Pasadena and they did not return to Germany but went to Belgium for a few months, where Queen Elizabeth and Einstein became better acquainted.

When offered several positions, Einstein decided to go to Princeton, N.J. They were joined by Elsa's daughter, Margot and her husband, Dmitri, until they divorced. Later, Maja, Einstein's sister, joined them from Italy. Secretary, Helen Dukas, remained as part of Einstein's household for the remainder of his life, and after his death she was the archivist of his papers.

In March 1928, Einstein collapsed with a heart condition, and was confined to bed for four months with an additional year spent recovering. Then during the 1930s, Einstein's personal life and health was shattered: his youngest son was committed to a hospital suffering from schizophrenia and a nervous breakdown,

Besso died who helped refine Einstein' ideas on his special theory of relativity, a close friend, Ehrenfest, committed suicide after killing his retarded son in 1933, and then Einstein suffered an even more devastating blow when Elsa died in 1936, his second wife of 20 years. Einstein was never as strong as before.

As World War II was proceeding in Europe, Szilard composed a letter for Einstein to send to President Roosevelt. Einstein sent a second letter to the President when it was obvious nothing was being done, informing him the Nazi were building a nuclear bomb. The United Nations set up a homeland for the Jewish people in Palestine, and Einstein was a supportive lecturer.

In 1948 and early 1949, Einstein was hospitalized with a large aneurysm of the abdominal aorta, a dilation the size of a grapefruit. After he was discharged, he spent a few weeks in Florida with Bucky to recover, and finished writing a short scientific biography.

Because of Einstein's pacifism and his support of Zionism, he was asked by Ben-Gurion in 1952 to consider the presidency of Israel. Einstein declined saying he was too naive in politics. He was also heard to say that equations were more important to him as politics were for the present but an equation was forever.

Einstein continued thinking, writing, and submitting scientific papers for publication, and writing introductions, forwards, and prefaces as requested. Einstein wrote and publish articles and books expressing his ideas, views, and opinions, during the last years of his life. His last three of four publications were making a clearer understanding of his gravitational theory in his general relativity theory.

In April of 1955, Einstein expressed his wish to die at home. The medical staff admitted him to the hospital at Princeton after their plea to him that his secretary could not care for him. Helen Dukas, his secretary, brought Einstein writing materials when he was in the hospital, and he continued his work on the unification theory. Einstein confided to his friend, Otto Nathan, the day before he died, that he was sure he was close to success. Einstein decided to put his papers down to rest on Sunday evening, and on Monday, 1:30 a.m., April 18, 1955, Einstein pass away of a burst aneurysm.

The world took notice and mourned the passing of a great man and an outstanding scientist.

Chapter 25

NUMBERS OF THE UNIVERSE AND THE UNIVERSE

Rees (1999) compiled six phenomenal numbers that if their concepts were changed only slightly that life and the universe as we know it would not be the same or even exist. It would take only a few less zeros, a difference of 1/100,000, or a change from 0.007 to 0.006 or to 0.008. It is the exactness of these numbers that we take for granted.

Rees' six numbers are: two related to the basic forces, two on the size and overall being of our universe, and two on the properties of space. All play an ultimate role in our universe. To some these numbers are a coincidence after the big bang, to some God maintaining the world, and to others just a combination of facts.

Hawking expressed that the laws of nature are delicate, and even a slight change in the physical laws can destroy life as we know it.

Hawking noted if the universe were to stop expanding and start contracting, it would eventually end up a singularity that is labeled by some as the big crunch.

Calder stated if our universe does collapse into a big crunch imagine a new universe being born out of the ashes in a new big bang.

It has been proposed that our universe may have enough dark energy to oppose gravity and thus cause continuous expansion. This would oppose the idea of a big crunch singularity at the end of the universe.

Calder mentioned religion may not enter into evaluating scientific evidence, but the religious urge to find the meaning of life certainly does.

ILLUSTRATIONS AND ILLUSTRATION CREDITS

ILLUSTRATIONS

Figure 1: Frontispiece: Painting of Albert Einstein. This painting is also the one on the back cover of this book.
Figure 2: Schwarzschild Black Hole
Figure 3: Kerr Black Hole
Figure 4: Painting of young Albert Einstein

LIST OF ILLUSTRATION CREDITS

Figure 1 is the frontispiece in this book that is a copy of the painting of Albert Einstein by Wieslaw Nowak, portrait painter and famous horse painter of Krakow, Poland, painted at the request of Robert Rinaldi. This same painting is also placed on the back cover of this book.

Figure 2 is an illustration of a Schwarzschild Black Hole, and Figure 3 is an illustration of a Kerr Black Hole. Both are designed and computerized by Robert Rinaldi with final computer images by Rita Kozlova Papas and Shirley Yee, with computer corrections by Anne Henderson Perkins.

Figure 4 is a copy of a painting of Albert Einstein as a young man by Polish artist, Wieslaw Nowak, painted at the request of Robert Rinaldi.

ACKNOWLEDGEMENTS

The authors wish to acknowledge our families for their forbearance and love, all our teachers and professors living and deceased including Jesus Muniz, Daniel Mazia, Cert Stern, Aharon Katchalski-Katzir, Richard Eakin, Heinz Holter, Howard Day, Bernard Abbott, Tom James, Loye Miller, and our colleauges and friends for guiding us through many storms and fair weather. We must confess, to mention any of them tends to reduce all of them and that is not our desire.

Grateful appreciation is extended to Anne Henderson Perkins for her computer assistance, and to Albert Einstein's biographers for their diligent research. Also, thank you to the Trafford publishing staff.

Sincerely,
Bob, Ivan and Barbara

SPECIAL MENTION

Manuel Hewitt honors his father, David, who's life was taken in an accident, and his proud grandfather, Paul Hewitt, as Manuel breaths atoms breathed by all beings before him. This is a perspective in time-space that exemplifies a truth for all.

Wieslaw and Barbara's "Mine Too" and Dan and Rebecca's Emma Margaret who were still born never making it into this world for us to love, share in their smiles and tears, and applaud their accomplishments.

To all: be thankful to God and use the opportunities you have, and eliminate waiting for tomorrow's tomorrow for life is now!

GLOSSARY

THIS GLOSSARY DOES NOT GIVE PRECISE DEFINITIONS, BUT GIVES THE CONCEPT OR INFORMATION TO HELP IN UNDERSTANTING. REMEMBER, ALL THE SCIENCES ARE CONTINUALLY CHANGING AND GROWING AS NEW RESEARCH IS ACCOMPLISHED AND INFORMATION IS DISCOVERED AND REVEALED.

absolute zero: The lowest possible temperature at which particles have no motion. On the Kelvin temperature scale absolute zero is 0°K. On the Celsius temperature scale it is minus 273.15°C. On the Fahrenheit temperature scale it is minus 459.69°F.

anomaly: Anomalies are deviations or departures from what has been proven to be correct or the expected usual results, such as probabilities that are frequent in the quantum theory. Green and Scherk working on the string theory for about four years came up with an infinity-free string theory that explained all four forces of the universe, elementary particles, and was anomaly-free. Witten using a different approach proved their theory was correct and anomaly-free.

antiparticle: An antiparticle has the same mass as the regular particle but an opposite charge. When a particle collides with its antiparticle, they annihilate each other leaving only energy/radiation. The antiparticle of the electron is the positron.

atom: An atom is the smallest particle of an element that has all of the element's chemical properties. An atom has a nucleus which contains protons and neutrons, and is surrounded by orbiting electrons. All atoms of a specific element are identical everywhere, here on earth and throughout the universe.

big bang: The big bang theory of the origin of the universe began with a singularity. In Einstein's 1916 general theory of relativity, he predicted that space-time began with a singularity. Friedman in 1922 and Lemaitre in 1927, published their views of an expanding universe, as did Gamow and Alpher in 1946. Hoyle named the origin of the universe "big bang" in 1948. In the 1960s, Penzias and Wilson's discovered radiation in all directions, and Dicke followed through with the satellite COBE's information and confirmation of temperatures to confirm the big bang origin of the universe.

big crunch: Einstein's general theory of space-time predicted that our planet would end in a big crunch singularity if it were to collapse and return to the rest of the universe.

black hole: Einstein and others noted the general theory of relativity described a stellar gravitational collapsing of stars, spinning and non-spinning, with a singularity at a finite point, and light not being emitted.

blue shift: When a star or other luminous object is viewed through a spectrograph with a prism, the elements it contains are in definite positions. If the line is shifted toward the blue end of the spectrum, this is called a blue shift noting the star or object is moving closer.

Bose-Einstein statistics: The Bose-Einstein statistics are an important and useful tool. Bose, using quantum concepts, developed a new type of statistics which Einstein improved showing it could be applied to atoms and molecules corrected to particles with a particular spin.

boson: The weak bosons are particles that are a force carrier involved in the weak nuclear force's interaction operation of decay. Massive bosons labeled as W+, W-, and Z° are carried by the weak nuclear force, and have a very short range.

brown dwarf: Brown dwarf stars emit no light and are completely cooled down iron white dwarf stars that previously emitted light.

Chandrasekhar limit: Chandrasekhar figured how big a star could be and still support itself against its own gravity after it had used up all its fuel. He calculated a cold star of more than one and a half times the mass of the sun could not be able to support itself against its own gravity; this is known as the Chandrasekhar limit. Stars above the limit when they come to the end of their fuel may explode or throw off enough matter to reduce their mass to avoid gravitational collapse as a black hole. If a star is less than the Chandrasekhar limit and a white dwarf when it runs out of light, it will eventually become a brown dwarf. Chandrasekhar showed that the exclusion principle (repulsion between neutrons and protons) could not stop the collapse of a star larger than the Chandrasekhar limit.

cosmic lens: Einstein's cosmic lens can be seen as the light from a star bends around dark matter or star aligned in front of it, magnifying the star. It is also called gravitational lensing.

cosmological constant: Einstein formulated his cosmological constant when writing his theory in 1914 to balance his equations when he believed in a static universe. He rejected his cosmological constant in 1927 when he realized the universe was not static but expanding. Astronomers are now using Einstein's cosmological constant to explain the expansion of the universe.

dark energy: Dark energy is also referred to as dark density. Dark energy may be the expansionary force that is opposing the gravitational force as the universe is expanding. Observed rotational velocities of stars on the outer regions of spiral galaxies is greater than the orbital velocities expected and could be due to dark energy.

dark matter: Dark matter is everywhere around and between the galaxies. It cannot be seen, but it is known to be there because of the influence of its gravitational field and gravitational lensing.

disorder: In physics, the behavior/disorder of atoms and molecules contained in isolated systems of quantum statistical mechanics is called entropy.

Doppler effect: The Doppler effect is the relationship between the frequency of the waves of light and the speed of the stars and galaxies. If the star or galaxy is moving away, the frequency of the waves will be lower, and if it is proceeding toward, the frequency of the waves will be higher. If the speed of the star or galaxy is moving away, the spectra will shift toward the red end of the spectrum (red shift), and if the speed of the star or galaxy is moving toward, the spectra will shift toward the blue end of the spectrum (blue shift). The Doppler effect is also known as the Doppler shift.

duality: Duality has different concepts of the same theory and may be useful for calculations in different kinds of situations. Einstein's lecture was the first clearly presented concept of duality when he explained light has dual properties as it can be a particle or it can be a wave, depending on the experiment. It can be a wave if it has a low energy beam and the wave length of the light beam is large, or it can be a particle if it has a high energy beam and the wave length of the light beam is small.

electrodynamics: Quantum electrodynamics has proven to be a successful theory. It describes many details of the electromagnetic interaction between charged particles.

116

electromagnetic force and electromagnetic field: Maxwell showed mathematically every electric charge and electric current is carried by a single field thereby electricity and magnetism are inseparable. Maxwell called the force electromagnetic force and the field that carries it electromagnetic field. The photons are the exchange particles which act on charged particles with infinite range in the electromagnetic force which holds atoms together.

electrons: Electrons are negative electrical charged particles in elliptic orbits around the nuclei of atoms. The size of the atom determines the attraction the positive charged nuclei have for the negative charged electrons. Bohr showed electrons orbit at certain specified distances from the nucleus within the atom.

energy: The total energy state of the universe is zero because matter is positive energy and the gravitational field is negative energy which neutralizes the positive energy of matter.

entropy: Clausius in 1865 coined the word entropy as a body similar to energy from the Greek word transformation when he was working with thermodynamics. The second law of thermodynamics states that entropy of an isolated system always increases, and when two systems are joined together, their entropy is greater than the sum of the individual systems. An alternative interpretation of entropy is used in quantum statistical mechanics in the statistical behavior/disorder of atoms and molecules contained in isolated systems.

ergospheres: The two ergospheres are the opening of the Kerr black hole beneath the static limit area. Once particles and light are in the ergospheres they precede to the event horizons, and then to the ring-shaped singularity in the center of the Kerr black hole. There are two ergospheres in the Kerr black hole that when they spin slowly they are separate and the spin is circular in shape, but as the spin increases the ergospheres merge and their spin is elliptical in shape.

escape velocity: The escape velocity is the velocity that an object needs to obtain and maintain to overcome the gravitational influence of the gravitational field in which it is located.

ether (luminiferous aether): Ether is a fixed medium that an electromagnetic phenomena, such as light or radio wave, can travel at a constant speed. Ether was tested by Michelson and Morley in 1887 to see if ether used in experiments was a benefit, made a difference, made variations in time detected, or made a change in the speed of light. The negative results obtained were against its usage.

event horizon: The event horizon is the entrance region into the black hole for particles and light. The Schwarzschild non-spinning black hole has one event horizon; but the Kerr spinning black hole has two event horizons that spin separately when spinning slow in a circular spin, but in a rapid spin, the two event horizons merge and the spin is an ellipse.

exchange particles: Exchange particles or particle interactions are the interactions of the four forces of the universe and their mediating field particles. The electromagnetic force is mediated by field particles called photons which are the quanta of the electromagnetic field and hold atoms together. The nuclear strong force is mediated by field particles called gluons and hold nuclei together. The weak nuclear force is mediated by particles called W±, Z, and bosoms, and is responsible for radioactive decay. The gravitational force is mediated by quanta of the gravitational field called gravitons that holds the universe together.

exclusion principle: The exclusion principle states that no two similar particles can have the same position and the same velocity. Pauli's exclusion principle states no two electrons in the same atom can be in the same quantum state, or have the same set of quantum numbers.

galaxy: A galaxy is a group of stars, interstellar matter and dark matter held together by gravity. The universe is composed of uncountable systems called galaxies that are millions of light years away. The Milky Way is the closest galaxy to the earth.

gamma rays: Gamma rays have wavelengths shorter than those of visible light. Gamma rays have no electrical charge, originate in the nucleus of radioactive elements, have electromagnetic radiation, and are high in frequency and energy. Radioactive elements emit three distinct types of rays: alpha rays with a positive electrical charge, beta rays with a negative electrical charge, and gamma rays that do not have a charge. Gamma rays include x-rays and ultraviolet light.

general relativity: General relativity refers to Einstein's general theory of relativity published in 1916 basically describing the force of gravity and the large scale structures of the universe. This general theory of 1916, his special theory of relativity of 1905, and his three other publications of 1905 set the scientific challenge of the nineteen hundreds.

gluons: Gluons are the exchange particles which act on particles called quarks of the strong nuclear force of the universe, and hold the nucleus together.

gravitational lensing: Einstein's gravitational lensing is produced by lining up two stars one directly in front the other. The star in front will bend the light rays of the star behind it, bending all wavelengths of the furthest star by the same amount. We then see a magnified image of the distant star with an image of the closer star in the center, and the furthest star appears as an Einstein ring. Lensing also works well when a black hole or dark matter is lined up directly in front of a star, and we see lensing and an Einstein ring.

gravitational radius: Schwarzschild calculated the singularity's radius for the sun, and it is referred to as the Schwarzschild radius or the gravitational radius.

graviton: Graviton is the exchange particle that acts on everything with an infinite range within the force of gravity which holds the solar system together.

gravitational waves: Gravitational waves were predicted by Einstein in 1918. Also that oscillating matter would create gravitational waves. Gravitational waves are weak compared to electromagnet waves, and difficult to detect. The Laser Interferometer Gravitation Wave Observatory's (LIGO) purpose is to detect gravitational waves; and other detectors are also searching to detect them.

gravity/gravitational force: Gravity is one of the four forces of the universe. It is the long-range force that dominates the universe over astronomical distances, and travels at the speed of light. Einstein changed the understanding of space-time, straight line, uniform gravity motion, to include all types of motion including curved-space gravity which he explained mathematically. Gravitons are the exchange particles that act on everything in the infinite range of the gravity force which holds the solar system together.

hadrons: Hadrons act with strong nuclear interactions over short distances with protons and neutrons that are bound together by the strong nuclear force that holds the nucleus together by repelling the huge electrical forces of repulsion that exists between the positively charged closely spaced protons. Protons of large nuclei are farther apart, and the electrical force of repulsion of the protons may be greater than the short range strong nuclear force, therefore, the large nuclei are not as stable as the heaver

120

elements. Hadrons and leptons are elementary particles of all mater except photons.

half-life: Half-life is the time required for half of an atom of a radioactive element to decay. The half-life of radioactive elements and elementary particles are constant for the rate of radioactive decay, and are not affected by external conditions such as temperature and pressure extremes, and magnetic fields. Half-life can be measured, and is determined from the rate of disintegration. The shorter the half-life of an element the faster is the rate of disintegration. The kinetic energy of a particle determines its wavelength that gives the probable state of the nucleus. Half-life can also be estimated using quantum mechanics.

Hubble's constant: Hubble's constant is a ratio of two numbers that are the recessional velocity of a galaxy divided by its distance.

infinity: Infinity is boundless, endless, unlimited, numberless, and eternal in some situations. There are infinities in the quantum theory and the string theory that involves renormalization by introducing new infinities to cancel the infinities that are in the theories.

interactions: All the interactions observed in the universe are by the four basic forces: gravity, electromagnetism, the strong nuclear force, and the weak nuclear force. Gravitons have an infinite range in the gravitational force that work on everything holding the solar system together. Gluons have a short range in the strong nuclear force working on quarks holding the nuclei together. Photons have infinite range in the electromagnetic force acting on charged particles holding atoms together. Bosons are short ranged particles in the weak nuclear force that act on electrons, neutrinos and quarks resulting in radioactive decay.

intermediate vector bosons: Intermediate vector bosons are exchange particles that act on quarks, electrons, and neutrinos of the weak nuclear force of the universe that result in radioactive decay.

isotopes: All of the isotopes of any one element go by the same name, the same symbol, all have the same nuclear charge, the same number of electrons per atom, the same atomic number, and the same chemical properties, but the only difference is the atomic mass. About three fourths of the elements have isotopes.

laser: The word laser stands for Light Amplification by Stimulated Emission of Radiation. Lasers are based on information that Einstein published in 1916 in three quantum papers of his discoveries of radiation transitions, stimulations, and emissions. Weber did some basic work in 1951, but it was Townes and Schawkiw working from 1951 to 1958 who published their laser paper, obtained a patent, but did not build a laser. The first laser was built by Maiman in 1960. Lasers are very versatile with some used in surgery in place of a knife, cutting and welding of metal in industry, and reading price tags at the checkout stands.

leptons: Leptons and hadrons are elementary particles which are building blocks of matter. Leptons are lighter particles composed of electrons or neutrinos.

light: Light travels at a finite, fast speed, and was studied and measured by Roemer in 1676. Michelson, in 1882, estimated the speed of light was 186,320 miles per second. Einstein explained the mathematical law of photoelectric effect in 1905, for which he received a Nobel Prize in Physics in 1921. A theory of how gravity affects light was done by Einstein in his general theory of relativity in 1916.

light energy: Light energy is a mass-less quantum particle called a photon. In the quantum theory, the higher the frequency of light, the greater is its energy content. For example, violet light has twice the frequency of red light, and one quantum of violet light has twice the energy content of one quantum of red light. The energy of a photon is greater at higher frequencies.

light year: The distance that light travels in one year is 5.878 trillion miles.

magnetic field: A magnetic field is the region that will interact with the magnetic properties of a magnet, or the region in the space about an electric charge in motion.

mass: Mass is a quantity used to measure the inertia of matter's resistance to a change in state of motion. Einstein realized that everything with mass has energy, even if not moving. Everything with energy has mass, even if not matter (solid, liquid, gaseous, and plasma) such as light and microwaves. The amount of energy (E) is related to the amount of mass (m) as in $E=mc^2$, known as the mass-energy equivalence.

microwave background radiation: Gamow and Alpher, and later Dicke and Peebles, predicted it, but Penzias and Wilson were given credit for discovering the radio energy called cosmic background radiation. The quantity of radiation is immense, and the same in every direction coming from outside our solar system. It was later confirmed by the satellite COBE's additional information. It is often referred to as cosmic background radiation.

naked singularity: The singularity of a gravitational collapsing star that occurs in a black hole where it is hidden by the event horizon. Naked singularity is a name given to a black hole's singularity when Penrose proposed his cosmic censorship hypothesis.

neutron: The neutron and the proton are held inside the nucleus by the strong nuclear force.

nuclear chain reaction: When set up properly the nuclear chain reaction is automatic. The problem is finding conditions a chain of reactions or cycle of reactions can maintain to assure the continuation of the release of energy at a predetermined rate. For example: a nuclear chain reaction in a nuclear fission process involves the capture of a neutron that results in the release of energy and simultaneously the release of neutrons. The mass of fissionable material has to be arranged to ensure the capture of the newly released neutrons and the dense neutrons' release of energy at the same time to lead to an explosive reaction. The ratio of these two numbers of neutrons is called the multiplication factor in chain reactions.

nuclear energy: In nuclear energy, binding energy is energy released when separate nucleons are combined to form a nucleus. In chemical reactions only a few electron volts of energy are released for every molecule formed in the process, while in nuclear reactions millions of electron volts of energy are released by each nucleus involved in the process. Nuclear energy is converted into products like heat and electricity, but the exception is in medical therapy where it is used directly and locally. Einstein's general theory of relativity and Einstein's $E=mc^2$ furnished tools for developing nuclear energy.

nuclear fission: Nuclear fission is the splitting of the heavy nucleus into two nuclei of elements with mass numbers 60 to 180. This was discovered by accident in 1934 by Fermi bombarding uranium with neutrons to produce elements which indicated a new process was taking place. Hahn and Strassmann found when uranium was bombarded by neutrons that a new uranium nucleus was formed by a neutron which was unstable and split into two nuclei now called nuclear fission. The energies released by neutrons in nuclear fission have a wide range. Nuclear fission was used to achieve the atomic bomb.

nuclear fusion: Nuclear fusion occurs naturally within the core of stars like our sun. To obtain energy similar to the process that fuels the sun, the fuel of hydrogen and energy is produced when hydrogen atoms fuse to create helium in a process called fusion. The exact complicated process of converting hydrogen to helium was worked out by Bethe. After two major problems were solved, a hydrogen bomb was made, tested twice but never used; and according to theory, there is no limit to its power.

nuclear reactors: Nuclear reactors are designed for many purposes, and the best source of radioactive isotopes for medical and industrial uses. Nuclear reactors are a source of energy for power plants or for conducting experiments. A nuclear reactor can be designed to maintain a self-sustained chain reaction, but the correct surface area to volume ratio is necessary for a sustained reaction to be achieved.

nucleus: The atom contains the nucleus and the orbiting electrons held together by the strong force. The nucleus is composed of electrically charged protons and electrically neutral neutrons. The positive charges of the protons are the same number as the negative charges of the orbiting electrons. The neutral uncharged neutrons account for half of the particles in the nucleus.

particle accelerator: A particle accelerator is a man made machine to accelerate charged particles giving them more energy so they can be studied and used in experiments. Rutherford was the first to think particle accelerators could reveal the nature of sub-atomic structure. He built positive and negative batteries at either end of a two meter glass tube with an electric current of electrons at the negative end to crash into the positive end. The CERN particle accelerator has a twenty kilometer long circular tunnel for the study of micro and subatomic particles.

particles and antiparticles: Dirac predicted in 1928 the electron had an anti-electron; and in 1932 the positron, the electron's antiparticle, was discovered. Every particle has an antiparticle and they have the same mass, same spin, but opposite charges. They are created or destroyed in equal numbers so the total electrical charge in the universe remains constant. This balance between matter and antimatter is called symmetry. The particles have a negative charge and the antiparticles have a positive charge. The time a particle and antiparticle exist is brief.

photon: Photons are the exchange particles that act on charged particles with an infinite range by the electromagnetic force which holds the atoms together. A photon in the quantum theory is a particle of light, or emission of radiation made up of particles Planck called quanta, and later called photon.

positron: A positron is a positively charged antiparticle of the electron.

proton: Atoms have a tiny nucleus made up of protons and neutrons which are inseparable. Protons contain two up quarks and one down quark. Neutrons contain two down quarks and one up quark. The nucleus is surrounded by orbiting electrons.

quanta: Planck, using quantum concepts, showed the emissions and absorption of a radiation curve for a heated object could be explained by using quantum quantities he called quanta, later called photons.

quantum chromo-dyamics (QCD): The quantum chromo-dynamic theory applies to the strong and weak nuclear reactions, and the particles called gluons that are exchanged between the quarks making up particles.

quantum electrodynamics (QED): Quantum electrodynamics describes the details of the electromagnetic interactions between charged particles, as in the exchange of photons. The quantum electrodynamic theory is very successful.

quantum jumps: Einstein published a paper on jumps between energy levels in which electrons would emit or absorb photons.

quantum mechanics (QME): The theory of quantum mechanics is based on Plank's quantum principle and the Heisenberg's uncertainty principle. The revised quantum theory is a quantum state which is a combination of position and velocity within the uncertainty principle.

quantum theory: Planck's radiation formula and quantum hypothesis of 1900 explained the observed rate of emission of radiation from hot bodies, and also worked very well with the microscopic studies in physics. Einstein assisted Planck in setting up the fundamentals, but Bohr's Copenhagen interpretation left Einstein questioning the theory's direction. Planck called the energy radiated in units, chunks of quantum.

quarks: Protons and neutrons are inside the nucleus and made up of smaller particles called quarks. Quarks are called up, down, strange, charmed, bottom and top, and come in red, green or blue. These color terms are just labels as quarks are much smaller than the wave length of visible light and do not have any color. A proton contains two up quarks and one down quark, while a neutron contains two down and one up quark. Particles can be made up of the other quarks (strange, charmed, bottom and top), but these have much greater mass, and decay rapidly into protons and neutrons.

radioactive decay: Radioactive decay is the breakdown or decay of atomic nuclei within the weak nuclear force affecting all matter particles, but not force carrying particles.

radioactivity: Becquerel in 1896 accidentally discovered uranium salt crystals emit an invisible radiation. This spontaneous emission of radiation was soon called radioactivity. Experiments by other scientists showed other substances were also radioactive, among the most notable were Pierre and Marie Curie discovering polonium and radium. Rutherford discovered three types of radiation can be emitted by a radioactive substance: alpha rays (emitted particles are Helium nuclei), beta rays (particles are either electrons or positrons) and gamma rays (high energy photons).

reaction: A chemical or energy reaction is a process of a rearrangement or exchange. Energy and mass can be changed but not destroyed. Chemical reactions are rarely more than a few electron volts, and only a few electron volts of energy are released for every molecule, but when millions of electron volts are released by each nucleus involved in a nuclear reaction, there is an enormous explosion. In medical therapy, radiation energy is used directly and locally in the form it is emitted. Large amounts of nuclear energy can be converted into heat in a nuclear reactor and then the heat can be converted into electricity.

red shift: When a star or other luminous object is viewed through a spectrograph with a prism, and the line shifts toward the red end of the spectrum, this is called a red shift, and the star or object is moving away from us. If the line is moving toward the blue end of the spectrum, this is a blue shift and the star or object is moving toward us.

singularity: A point in space-time that the space-time curvature is or becomes infinite as in the big bang theory. A singularity at a finite radius is different as Oppenheimer showed it had a physical relevance when applied to a collapsing star (black hole}. This is similar to Schwarzschild's singularity in a black hole being a point, and the singularity in a spinning Kerr black hole being a circle.

singularity theorem: A theorem that the universe started with a singularity such as in the big bang theory. Penrose's theorem showed that any collapsing star must end in a singularity; and Hawking, by reversing time, proved the expanding universe must have begun with a singularity.

space-time: Einstein's general theory of relativity combines space and time, with all things existing in four dimensions:

three dimensions of space (length, width and height), and one dimension of time. Physicists call this the space-time continuum.

special relativity: Special relativity refers to Einstein's special theory of relativity published in 1905. He published three other papers in the same year that helped change the field of physics.

spectroscope: A spectroscope is an optical instrument that separates light into its frequencies in the form of spectral lines. If the lines are in a particular position, the elements in the object can be determined, and also its temperature. When the lines move to one end or the other end of the spectrum, it can be determined if the object is moving toward or away from us.

spectrum: A spectrum is the array of wavelengths composing light from a star or object as seen using a spectroscope. White light when passed through a prism is separated into a band of colors into a spectrum. The colors in a spectrum of an object depend on the wavelengths of light the object reflects.

speed of light: The speed of light is 186,000 miles per second.

spin: A rotational momentum possessed by certain objects and particles.

static limit area: In black holes, the static limit area is where the collapsing star's particles or light cannot remain at rest.

stimulated emissions: Einstein theoretically figured the coherence of atomic light could be achieved giving off light of a particular frequency that would attract another particle of light of the same frequency resulting in stimulation of emission of radiation. Einstein's 1916 discovery of the coherence of atomic light of stimulated emissions of radiation was not utilized until 1959 when it was used in the invention and versatile manufacture of the laser in 1960.

string theory: The string theory of physics has undergone many stages of development since its inception. Presently, the M-theory is composed of six string theories, ten coiled up dimensions connected by dualities, and containing all of the four forces of the universe. Energy is obtained from the vibrating motion and the winding energy of the one dimensional (length) strings from which the original theory got its name.

strong nuclear force: The strong nuclear force is the strongest of the four forces of the universe, has the shortest range, holds protons and neutrons together inside the nuclei of the atom, and can overcome the electromagnetic force. The strong nuclear force's exchange particle is gluon with particles that act on quarks.

superfluidity: Einstein using the Bose-Einstein statistics predicted a Bose-Einstein condensate phenomenon at absolute zero where atoms would overlap and coalesce into a macroscopic wave packet, a new form of matter different from solids, liquids and gases. Einstein called it superatom, and later was called superfluidity. Years later it was verified when temperature close to absolute zero could be obtained.

supergravity: Supergravity is an eleven-dimensional theory by Kaluza and Klein. Witten showed there was a connection between the five superstring theories with eleven dimensions and supergravity's eleven dimensions resulting in six theories in the M-theory using dualities.

supersymmetry: In Wess and Zumino's theory, supersymmetry is a symmetry in which bosons and fermions are two states of the same particle. They found that the supersymmetry theory predicted that every particle that transmits forces has a matter particle partner called superpartner. By applying symmetry principles, they could mathematically

130

change bosons to fermions and vice versa. In the supersymmetric theory, the positive and negative energies cancel out completely so there is no amount of energy lost or gained. With the addition of supersymmety, the string theory became known as the superstring theory, and later, with the addition of supergraviity, it became the M-theory.

thermodynamics: Carnot in 1832, considered the founder of thermodynamics, stated energy can only be altered in form. Kelvin confirmed and extended thermodynamics in 1850.

     The concept of internal energy is involved in the first law as an increase in one form of internal energy must be accompanied by a decrease in some other form of energy such as heat added or expended. In 1865, Clausius proposed entropy as a variable to go along with the internal energy, pressure, volume and temperature.

     In the second law of thermodynamics, the energy (entropy/disorder) of a system always increases, and when two systems are joined together, the energy (entropy/disorder) of the combined system is greater than the sum of the individual systems.

     The concept of temperature is involved in the Zeroth law of thermodynamics as when two bodies are in thermal equilibrium with a third body then the first two bodies will be in thermal equilibrium with each other if placed in thermal contact (also known as the law of equilibrium).

uncertainty principle: Heisenberg's uncertainly principle was combined into the quantum mechanic theory stating there is probability when measuring two or more variables simultaneously. Certain variables such as position and velocity or momentum can not be simultaneously measured to a high degree of accuracy in quantum mechanics.

unified field theory (UFT): A theory unifying gravitation and electromagnetic fields, often called the theory of everything (TOE), or the grand unified theory (GUT). Einstein tried to formulate quantum mechanics with his general theory of relativity without success.

universe: At first the universe was thought to be flat. In 340 B.C., Aristotle and the mariners realized the earth was spherical, but thought the earth was stationary with the sun, moon, planets and stars moving in circular orbits above the earth. In the second century, Ptolemy wrote the earth was the center and the planets moved in circles in their own spheres. Copernicus in 1514 wrote the sun was the stationary center with the earth and planets moving in circular orbits around the sun. Galileo in 1609, viewing with a telescope, wrote the earth was the stationary center of the universe; and he was the first to report the planet Jupiter's moons. Kepler in 1610 suggested that Copernicus was correct, but the planets did not move in circles but in ellipses; and reported there were fixed stars that did not change positions. In 1684, Newton published how cosmic bodies moved, suggested a law of universal gravitation, and stated the universe was not static as previously believe. Olbers also suggested the universe was not static in 1823. Hubble in 1929, and others (Friedmann and Lemaitre) before him, proved the universe was moving and expanding.

virtual pairs: In quantum mechanics, a particle and its antiparticle can annihilate one another and release gamma ray photons (matter to energy); and the high energy of the gamma rays or photons can be exchanged to quickly produce a particle and antiparticle (energy to matter) in pair production. They cannot be observed but do have measurable effects. They are sometimes called virtue pairs, virtual particles and virtual antiparticles.

wavelength: A wavelength is the distance between wave crests and troughs. A wavelength of visible light is between forty and eighty millionths of a centimeter.

132

waves: Waves with wavelengths shorter than those of visible light are known as gamma rays, x-rays, and ultraviolet light. Waves with wavelengths longer than those of visible light are known as radio waves, microwaves and infrared radiation.

weak nuclear force: The weak nuclear force is one of the four forces of the universe. The intermediate vector bosons, gauge bosons, and W± and Z bosons are exchange particles that act on quarks, electrons, and neutrinos in the short range weak nuclear force. The weak nuclear force is responsible for radioactive decay, the decay of particles created in accelerators, and the decay of cosmic rays. The weak nuclear force was discovered by Fermi.

wormhole: A wormhole is space becoming so warped that it bends back on itself creating a bridge through space-time. In 1935, Einstein and Rosen studied the space around the gravitational radius in the Einstein Rosen bridges. Droste found a funnel shaped tunnel that lead to the gravitational radius. Einstein discovered a mirror image tunnel on the other end. These tunnels became known as Einstein-Rosen bridges, and later called wormholes in space. Wormholes are also in black holes as a possible means of the singularity and matter to escape into the universe through the white hole.

BIBLIOGRAPHY

THIS IS A LIST OF THE REFERENCES MANY THAT ARE TREASURED TO READ AGAIN, SOME OWNED, SOME BORROWED, SOME FROM THE LIBRARY, SOME GLANCED THROUGH, SOME PONDERED OVER, AND SOME READ AGAIN AND AGAIN. THE LIST TO US OPENED DOORS OF INSIGHT, AND WE ARE GRATEFUL TO THE WRITERS WHO SPENT MONTHS AND YEARS WRITING THEM TO RECORD THE THOUGHTS OF THEIR SUBJECTS, THEIR OWN THOUGHTS, AND MOST IMPORTANTALLY THE FACTS OF SCIENCE AND PHYSICS.

Albert, David Z. *Quantum Mechanics and Experience.* Massachusetts: Harvard University Press, 1992.

Atkins, Peter. *Four Laws that Drive the Universe.* Oxford, England: Oxford University Press, 2007.

___. *Physical Chemistry.* 5th ed. New York: Freeman, 1994.

Bergamini, David, and Editors of Life. *Mathematics.* New York: Time, 1963.

Bodanis, David. *E=mc²: A Biography of the World's Most Famous Equation.* New York: Walker, 2000.

Bohm, David. *Quantum Theory.* New York: Prentice-Hall, 1951.

Bolles, Edmond Blair. *Einstein Defiant: Genius vs. Genius in the Quantum Revolution.* Washington, DC: Henry of Academies, 2004.

Bondi, Hermann. *Relativity and Common Sense: A New Approach to Einstein.* Garden City: Anchor of Doubleday, 1964.

Born, Max. *Einstein's Theory of Relativity.* New York: Dover,

1965.

___. *The Restless Universe.* New York: Dover, 1951.

Boslough, John. *Stephen Hawking's Universe, An Introduction to the Most Remarkable Scientist of Our Time.* New York: Avon of Hearst, 1985.

Brian, Denis. *Einstein: A Life.* New York: Wiley, 1996.

Calaprice, Alice. *The Einstein Almanac.* Maryland: John Hopkins University Press, 2005.

___. *The Expanded Quotable Einstein.* New Jersey: Princeton University Press, 2002.

Calder, Nigel. *Einstein's Universe: Relativity Made Plain.* New York: Viking, 1984.

Carrol, Sean. *Dark Matter, Dark Energy: The Dark Side of the Universe.* Chantilly, VA: Teaching Company, 2007.

Cassirer, Ernst. *Substance and Function and Einstein's Theory of Relativity.* New York: Dover, *1953.*

Chaisson, Eric, and Steve McMillan. *Astronomy Today.* Englewood Cliffs: Prentice-Hall of Simon and Schuster, 1993.

Cheniot, Denis, et al. *Singularity Theory: Dedicated to Jean-Paul Braselet.* Hackensack: World Scientific, 2007.

Clark, Ronald W. *Einstein: The Life and Times.* New York: Avon of Harpers Collins, 1971.

___. *Einstein, The Life and Times: an Illustrated Biography.* Avenel: Wings of Random House, 1984.

Clark, Stuart. *Stars and Atoms from the Big Bang to the Solar System.* New York: Oxford University Press, 1995.

Daintith, John, and Dered Gjertsen, eds. *Oxford Dictionary of Scientist* 2d ed. New York: Oxford University Press, 1999.

Davies, Paul. *About Time: Einstein's Unfinished Revolution.* New York: Touchstone of Simon and Schuster, 1995.

Dukas, Helen and Banesh Hoffmann, eds. *Albert Einstein: The Human Side, New Glimpses from His Archives.* New Jersey: Princeton University Press, 1981.

Einstein, Albert. *Ideas and Opinions.* New translations and revisions by Sonja Bargmann. Edited by Carl Seelig. Reprint. New York: Wing Books of Random House, 1955

___. *Letters to Solovine.* Translated by Wade Baskin. New York: Philosophical Library, 1987.

___. *Out of My Later Years.* New York: Citadel Press of Carol,

1991.

___. *Relativity: The Special and the General Theory.* Translated by Robert W. Lawson from the 1906 ed. in 1916. Reprint. New York: Wings of Random House, 1961.

___. *The Meaning of Relativity Including the Relativistic Theory of the Non Symmetric Field.,* 5th ed. Translated by Edwin Pimperton Adams from the 1916 ed. in 1922, Appendix I for the 3d ed. in 1945 translated by Ernst G. Straus, and Appendix II for in the 5th ed. in 1954 translated by Sonja Bargmann. Reprint. New Jersey: Princeton University Press, 1956.

___. *The World as I See It.* Translated by Alan Harris. Secaucus: Citadel Press of Carol, 1997.

Einstein, Albert, and Bruria Kaufman. *"Algebraic Properties of the Field in the Relativistic Theory of the Asymmetric Field."* Annals of Mathematics 59 (1954): 230-44.

___. *"A New Form of the General Relativistic Field Equations."* Annals of Mathematics 62 (1955): 128-38.

Eisenstaedt, Jean. *The Curious History of Relativity: How Einstein's Theory of Gravity Was Lost and Found Again.* Translated by Arturo Sangalli. New Jersey: Princeton University Press, 2006.

Feldman, Burton. *112 Mercer Street: Einstein, Russell, Godel, Pauli, and the End of Innocence in Science.* Edited and completed by Katherine Williams. New York: Arcade, 2007.

Ferris, Timothy, ed. *The World Treasury of Physics, Astronomy, and Mathematics.* New York: Back Bay Books of Little and Brown, 1991.

Feynman, Richard P. *Feynman's Thesis: A New Approach to Quantum Theory.* Edited by Laurie M. Brown. New Jersey: World Scientific, 2005.

___. *Six Easy Pieces.* New York: Basic Books of Perseus, 1963.

___. *Six Easy Pieces and Six Not-So-Easy Pieces.* Massachusetts: Perseus, 1997.

___. *The Feynman Lectures on Physics: Vol. I, II, and III.* Edited by R. B. Leighton and M. Sands. Reading: Pearson of Addison-Wesley, 2006.

Feynman, Richard P., Michael A. Gottlieb, and Ralph Leighton. *Feynman's Tips on Physics.* New York: Pearson of

Addison-Wesley, 2006.

Filkin, David. *Stephen Hawking's Universe.* New York: Basic Books of Harper Collins, 1997.

Ford, Kenneth W. *The Quantum World: Quantum Physics for Everyone.* Massachusetts: Harvard University Press, 2004.

French, A. P., ed. *Einstein: A Centenary Volume.* Massachusetts: Harvard University Press, 1979.

Goldsmith, Donald, and Robert Libbon. *The Ultimate Einstein.* New York: Pocket Books of Simon and Schuster, 1997.

Greene, Brian. *The Elegant Universe: Super Strings, Hidden Dimensions, and the Quest for the Ultimate Theory.* New York: Norton, 1999.

___. *The Fabric of the Cosmos, Space, Time and the Texture of Reality.* New York: Knop, 2004.

Greenstein, George. *Frozen Star.* New York: Freundlich Books, 1983.

Gribbin, John. *Unveiling the Edge of Time: Black Holes, White Holes, Wormholes.* New York: Harmony Books, 1992.

Harman, Peter Michael. *Energy, Force, and Matter.* New York: Cambridge University Press, 1982.

Harrison, Edward R. *Cosmology: The Science of the Universe.* New York: University of Cambridge Press, 1981.

Hawking, Stephen. *A Brief History of Time from the Big Bang to Black Holes.* London: Bantam Press of Transworld, 1988.

___. *A Stubbornly Persistent Illusion: The Essential Scientific Works of Albert Einstein.* Philadelphia: Running Press, 2007.

___. *The Universe in a Nutshell.* New York: Bantam Books of Random House, 2001.

Hawking, Stephen, and Leonard Mlodinow. *A Briefer History of Time.* New York: Bantam Dell of Random House, 2005.

Hawkins, Michael. *Hunting Down the Universe: The missing mass, primordial black holes, and other dark matters.* Reading: Helix Books of Addison-Wesley, 1997.

Hewitt, Paul G. *Conceptual Physics.* 6th ed. New York: Harper Collins, 1989.

Holton, Gerald. *Einstein: History and Other Passions.* Woodbury: American Institute of Physics, 1995.

Kaku, Michio. *Einstein's Cosmos: How Albert Einstein's Vision Transformed Our Understanding of Space and Time.*

New York: Atlas Books of Norton, 2004.

___. *Physics of the Impossible.* New York: Doubleday, 2008.

Kaler, James B. *Stars and Their Spectra.* New York: Cambridge University Press, 1989.

Kaufmann, William. *Universe.* 4th ed. New York: Freeman, 1994.

Kirshner, Robert P. *The Extravagant Universe.* New Jersey: Princeton University Press, 2002.

Krauss, Lawrence M. *Atom.* New York: Back Bay Books of Little and Brown, 2002.

Layzer, David. *Constructing the Universe.* New York: Freeman, 1984.

Lerner, Eric. *The Big Bang Never Happened.* New York: Times Books of Random House, 1991.

Lindley, David. *End of Physics; The Myth of a Unified Theory.* New York: Basic Books of Perseus, 1993.

Munowitz, Michael. *Knowing: The Nature of Physical Law.* New York: Oxford University Press, 2005.

Murphy, James T., James M. Hollon, and Paul W. Zitewitz. *Physics: Principles and Problems.* Columbus: Merrill of Bell and Howell, 1972.

Pagels, Heinz R. *Perfect Symmetry: The Search for the Beginning of Time.* New York: Bantam Books, 1991.

Pais, Abraham. *Subtle is the Lord: The Science and the Life of Albert Einstein.* New York: Oxford University Press, 1982.

Panek, Richard, *"The Year of Albert Einstein."* Smithsonian Magazine (June 2005): 108-19.

Parker, Barry. *Albert Einstein's Vision: Remarkable Discoveries that Shaped Modern Science.* Amherst: Prometheus Books, 2004.

Polkinghorne, John C. *The Particle Play: An account of the ultimate Constituents of Matter.* San Francisco: Freeman, 1981.

Rees, Martin. *Before the Beginning: Our Universe and Others.* Reading: Helix of Addison-Wesley, 1997.

___. *Just Six Numbers: The Deep Forces that Shape the Universe.* New York: Basic Books, 2000.

Resnick, Robert. *Introdction to Special Relativity.* New York: Wiley and Sons, 1968.

Rigden, John S. *Einstein 1905: The Standard of Greatness.* Massachusetts: Harvard University Press, 2005.

Robinson, Andrew. *Einstein: A Hundred Years of Relativity.* New York: Abrams, 2005.

Rosenkranz, Ze'Ev. *The Einstein Scrapbook.* Maryland: John Hopkins University Press, 1998.

Sagan, Carl. *Cosmos.* New York: Random House, 1980.

Sanders, Frederick A., and Paul Kirkpatrick. *College Physics.* 4th ed. New York: Holt, 1953.

Segre, Emilio. *From X-Rays to Quarks: Modern Physicists and Their Discoveries.* New York: Freeman, 1980.

Semat, Henry, and Harvey E. White. *Atomic Age Physics.* New York: Rinehart, 1959.

Serway, Raymond A., and Jerry S. Faughn. *College Physics.* 3th ed. Orlando: Saunders of Harcourt Brace, 1992.

Shipman, Harry L. *Black Holes, Quasars, and the Universe.* Boston: Houghton Mifflin, 1976.

Sugimoto, Kenji. *Albert Einstein: A Photographic Biography.* Translated by Barbara Harshav. New York: Schocken, 1989.

Sullivan, Walter. *Black Holes, The Edge of Space, The End of Time.* Garden City: Anchor Press of Doubleday, 1979.

Susskind, Leonard, and James Lindesay. *An Introduction to Black Holes, Information and the String Theory Revolution.* Hackensack: World Scientific, 2005.

Trefil, James S. *Space, Time, Infinity: The Smithsonian Views the Universe.* New York: Pantheon Books of Random House, 1985.

___. *The Moment of Creation: Big Band Physics from Before the First Millisecond to the Present Universe.* New York: Scribner's Sons, 1983.

Tyson, Neil de Grasse. *Death by Black Hole, and Other Cosmic Quandaries.* New York: Norton, 2007.

Wolf, Fred Alan. *Taking the Quantum Leap.* New York: Harper and Row, 1989.

World Almanac and Book of Facts. 10th ed. Edited by Sarah Janssen. (New York: World Almanac Books, 2011), 440-443, s.v.v. "Nobel Prizes in Physics and Chemistry".

INDEX OF NAMES

143

INDEX OF TOPICS

What was–WAS!

What is–IS!

What will be–WILL BE!